The Moral Foundations of Business Practice

James B. Wilbur

S.U.N.Y. College at Geneseo, Emeritus

For the fact seems to be that the really great corporation managements have reached a position for the first time in their history in which they must consciously take account of philosophical considerations. They must consider the kind of community in which they have faith, and which they will serve, and which they intend to help construct and maintain. In a word, they must consider at least in its more elementary phases the ancient problem of the "good life", and how their operations in the community can be adopted to affording or fostering it.

Adolf A. Berle—20th Century Capitalist Revolution

UNIVERSITY PRESS OF AMERICA

Lanham
New York
London

University Press of America®, Inc.
4720 Boston Way
Lanham, Maryland 20706

3 Henrietta Street
London WC2E 8LU England

Printed in the United States of America
British Cataloging in Publication Information Available

Library of Congress Cataloging-in-Publication Data

Wilbur, James Benjamin.
The moral foundations of business practice / by James B. Wilbur.
p. cm.
Includes bibliographical references and index.
1. Business ethics. I. Title.
HF5387.W52 1992 174'.4—dc20 92–6277 CIP

ISBN 0–8191–8650–3 (cloth : alk. paper)
ISBN 0–8191–8651–1 (paper : alk. paper)

™ The paper used in this publication meets the minimum requirements of American National Standard for Information Sciences—Permanence of Paper for Printed Library Materials, ANSI Z39.48–1984.

For Margie,
Sine qua non.

Acknowledgements

To begin with, my thanks and appreciation to David A. Martin, then Head of The School of Business at Geneseo, for the invitation and the room to begin these reflections. Whether he approves of their result is another matter entirely, but I owe him much.

Thanks go to the following for allowing me to use materials from their publications, as stated here and referenced within:

W. Michael Hoffman, Director, Center for Business Ethics, Bentley College, for the use of my "The Foundations of Corporate Responsibility" in his *Proceedings of the Second National Conference on Business Ethics : Power and Responsibility in the American Business System*, Washington, D.C.: University Press of America, 1979, pp. 235-250. Here, pieces of it are scattered throughout but, largely, in Chapters One and Five. Also, for the use of my "Corporate Character" in his *Corporate Governance and Institutionalizing Ethics : Proceedings of the Fifth National Conference on Business Ethics*, Lexington, MA : D.C. Heath and Company, 1984, pp. 173-184, which, with minor changes, constitutes Chapter Nine.

Borg-Warner Corporation, for the use of "The Beliefs of Borg-Warner : To Reach Beyond the Minimal," Chicago, IL : Borg-Warner Corporation, 1982, as referenced in Chapter Five.

Basil Blackwell, Inc., for referenced quotations in Chapter Five from *Individualism and Public Life : A Modern Dilemma*, by Ralph Ketcham, New York : Basil Blackwell, Inc., 1987.

I want to thank Pam Thomas of the Department of Philosophy for her typing of the various versions over the years and for the transition to, and most of what I know about, computerland.

Finally, appreciation and thanks, over and above the Dedication, are due to my wife, Margie, whose faith is sustaining and whose editorial capacities and sense of good usage have improved the whole.

J.B.W.
Manchester, Vt.

Table of Contents

Preface

For the past seven or eight years my concern has been with developing an undergraduate college course in Ethics and Management for our School of Business at Geneseo. My background for this activity lies in twenty-five years of study and teaching in the history of ideas including but not limited to the field of ethics. That a philosopher should be allowed to run loose in the field of business studies let alone to teach a required course in the management degree program is indicative of the fundamental questioning going on in our country of the traditional, classical and, in large measure, successful ideas and institutions of business practice. Simply and aptly put, the focus of this questioning lies in the title of Leonard Silk and David Vogel's excellent little book, *Ethics and Profits: The Crisis in Confidence in American Business*, and it has to do with the legitimacy of business practice, especially of the corporate variety, within the larger framework of our society. The authors point out that —

> to talk of the business corporation as facing a "crisis of legitimacy" does not imply that there exists any significant controversy as to whether it should exist; there is not. Rather it is to suggest that corporate leaders are being confronted with two basic questions: By what right do you who manage these huge corporations exercise your power? And what means do we have to insure that corporate power will be exercised in accord with some generally accepted notion of the public interest?[1]

Under normal, everyday circumstances the average person cannot exercise his power in ways harmful to large numbers of people. Every so often someone goes berserk and kills several people but these are exceptions and harm only a limited number. We do our best most of the time to limit such possibilities but the freedom accorded the citizens of our communities maintains that possibility. And when such things do come about and we reflect on them, we are properly appalled but powerless to prevent without curtailing all liberty and personal freedom. Within such limits we are all at the mercy of the civility and self-government of the individual. Of course, our elected officials exercise large powers over the community and we are quite careful with our legal descriptions of such powers and guidelines for their exercise.

In the last analysis and beyond the courts, the ballot box can remove what it bestowed. But corporate executives also exercise powers directly affecting the whole community. How can the public effects of the private exercise of power be made legitimate? Milton Friedman, as one of his arguments against the "social responsibilities" of business executives, makes the point that such social responsibility would be public in nature and the job of our system of elected officials at whatever level. Such concerns are outside the function of management in private enterprise. This is certainly an important point to consider. The marking off of the "public" and the "private" is one of the issues arising in the question of legitimacy, quoted above, in most telling ways. Private enterprise is no longer only a matter of private property, if it ever was, and the justification of the power wielded is a real problem for those who suffer it. The creation of benefits involves risks and some suffering, and what limitations should be placed upon private enterprise, in the name of the community, is a difficult matter and varies with time and circumstance. Mining conditions and pollution are obvious examples but so are the company store, cut-throat competition and harassment at work. There is also an historical aspect of this that must be mentioned.

With the disappearance of the frontier at the end of the last century, the era of rugged individualism, which characterized our settling years, came to an end. I have a movie memory of granite-jawed Spencer Tracy astride his horse surrounded by thousands of acres of the great southwest that he has acquired by guile or guts. His control of it all is threatened by oncoming settlers and this pressure of people has modified and in some degree civilized our social framework as far as natural individual persons are concerned. But just how this civilizing process is to be applied to those artificial, corporate persons of the business community that were originally modeled upon the rugged or atomic individual and are collectively referred to as "free enterprise," is not yet clear. Socially, rugged individualism is no longer given foot-room or appreciated. We have come to call the leaders of the business community at the close of last century who founded many of our corporations and large fortunes, "robber barons," a term of opprobrium covering the acquisitiveness and the methods employed to attain the ends of the most successful of these early pioneers in big business. Within our own century the growth of publicly owned corporations, the development of professional management and the increasing determination of the public to regulate business activity by means of laws and government agencies have done much to mitigate the atomic individualism of the earlier era. But the idea of the single-minded, hard driving, business entrepreneur is still a large part of the business ideal. In our own day, almost a century later, the emphasis has turned away from managerial structures and back to entrepreneurship, the value and importance of the individual in our information oriented society. It will be interesting to see how our contemporary conceptions of the entrepreneur compare with the rugged individualism of the robber barons. It will become clear in what is presented here that all our efforts are on the civilizing side but very much centered on the individual. And this is not merely a problem for business. It covers American culture. There is a general conviction among many of us that our traditional individualism in the frontier world is in large part responsible for our achievements as a people. It is next to impossible to deny a large measure of truth in this conviction, even if you think of some of those achievements themselves, or, at least some of their consequences, as unfortunate. The aura and fable surrounding the idea of the entrepreneur is an apposite example.

Philosophically, the ethic of practice put forward here owes very much to Kant's Practical Reason and to the Pragmatism of C.I. Lewis. From one perspective this book constitutes an application, with significant modifications, of Kantian classical liberalism to the American experience primarily in the area of business practice but involving the political and the individual as well. With these general remarks as background, let me proceed with a summary statement of the argument as it is developed.

In the Introductory Chapter, the question of the foundations of moral responsibility and its application to corporations is laid out and the corporate, managerial and individual levels of the inquiry distinguished. Several current perspectives on corporate responsibility are presented as context for the thesis that corporate activity can best be understood on analogy with the activity of persons and several good reasons for taking the analogy seriously are given. First, moral responsibility must be established at the level of individual practice and then we must decide in what sense, if any, such moral responsibility can be applied to the corporate level.

Chapter Two, Practice and Its Presuppositions, sets out the characteristics of practice based upon an analysis of activity borrowed from Albury Castell's *The Self in Philosophy*. Castell makes the point that, beyond doubting, there are activities because their denial is itself an activity. This is a "pragmatic contradiction" and we shall return to this self-referential argument later on as a central consideration of practice. Then, we inquire into the presuppositions of practice, the enabling conditions that form a common ground of concern for anybody's practice. One of these is seen to be freedom of choice that carries the possibility of destroying these preconditions through wrong choice. Morality will be understood as the concern for the establishment and maintenance of these common enabling conditions of all practice. Practice is also seen to be bi-polar and this divides the enabling conditions into two sets of three; *choice, concern* and *consistency* for the inner or Self pole and *multiplicity, continuity* and *structure* for the outer or World pole. Throughout, we shall take practice to be basic, that is, prior to theory, as an existing condition and some of the implications of this will become important for how we think about the problems considered.

Chapter Three, The Dimensions of Practice, analyses first, the Acquisitive dimension, having to do with the purposive suiting of means to ends, and then, the Maintenance dimension, having to do with the enabling conditions and their function. Traditional consequential eithical theories, such as Utilitarianism, place primary emphasis upon the Acquisitive dimension while a duty-centered ethic, notably, the Kantian ethic, centers upon the Maintenance dimension. I do not believe that the Acquisitive, with its concern for consequences, can furnish any foundation for the moral "ought." But the means-ends concern of the Acquisitive is essential to the coming into being of the moral in that only when some end is being pursued do any moral considerations come up at all. The Acquisitive is the occasion of the moral.

The Maintenance dimension is concerned with the enabling conditions, with the non-consequential and the non-linear aspects of practice. I have used my understanding of Kant to explain this dimension. But, as will be seen, practice cannot accept Kant's mutually exclusive separation between the moral and the prudential. The difference between the two dimensions is explained in terms of Aristotle's distinction between the actualizing of a potential and the exercise of a capacity. The problem of the relation between the two and the unity of them in just practice will be looked into later on. Some examples of the functioning of the enabling conditions in practice are given with reference to the classroom, the family and in conversation. They are also used to criticize Friedman's famous view of the responsibility of corporate executives, to lend credence to Adam Smith's Invisible Hand, to interpret Madison's phrase, "the permanent and aggregate interests of the community," and, finally, to make a comparison between our traditional economic and political systems.

In Chapter Four, The Enabling Conditions: Applications I, the purpose is to show what the enabling conditions will support as foundation. Three contemporary studies of individualism are used: *Habits of the Heart*, centering upon the need for community, *Individualism and Public Life*, centering upon the need for public concern and *Ethics and Profits*, centering upon the need for public trust. The point with each is that only an adequate notion of self-interest, one that includes the enabling conditions can meet the problems raised in these studies.

Chapter Five continues the application of these enabling conditions as foundations for a theory of rights, the theory of contract, the conditions of the free market and the nature of regulation. Two existing codes of ethics, one legal and the other corporate, are considered as embodiments of the analysis of practice being developed.

Chapter Six is concerned with how norms arise in practice, the hypothetical and categorical norms of the two dimensions and the relation between these two dimensions traditionally called the prudential and the moral. The possibility of norms is seen to reside in the reflective and self-referential character of consciousness. Within the goal-oriented dimension of practice, the means required for completion constitute the operational norms for the Acquisitive dimension and are hypothetical in nature and, traditionally, come under prudence. The limitations arising from practice itself, the enabling conditions, no matter what goal is chosen, constitute the norms of the Maintenance dimension, are categorical in nature and come under the moral. The relationship between the two is considered in terms of Kant's earlier and later views, involving first, separation and then, subordination and finally, a suggestion of his is developed for a reciprocal and organic relationship. To exemplify how interconnected the two dimensions are in practice, an example of running a news-stand is analyzed. In an ethic of practice, it is possible to distinguish the two dimensions but not to separate them. Not only is the acquisitive the occasion of the moral but the concern of the moral in practice extends beyond the inner conditions of maintenance to the outer conditions of the world and a general concern for consequences. The idea of "prudence" is used to present this extension. To illustrate how the moral relates to the complexity of practice, the various formulations of the categorical imperative found in Kant are related to practice and the version used in this work can be seen to emphasize its self-referential character and its consistent application in practice by anyone rather than its universalizability. The fact that these two dimensions of practice can be in conflict, as in a pragmatic contradiction, underlies the notions of right and wrong practice and forms the foundation for the meaning of just practice.

In Chapter Seven, Justice and the Scope of the Moral, the two concerns of Justice, equality and desert, are seen to be based upon the two dimensions of practice. Justice is not only a matter of the rights of individuals comparatively but also with how those protected capacities have been used by individuals in the matter at hand. In an ethic of practice, a just practice is one that is consistent with its own possibility, one in which the two dimensions are not out of joint but compatible. Over and above the instrumental use of reason in the means-end sphere of practice, reason participates in determining ends for practice in terms of the limiting conditions that constrain practice.

Chapter Eight, Self-Reference and the Categorical in Practice, begins by contrasting logical with pragmatic contradiction. The latter is characterized as self-refuting founded upon an irreducible conflict between the poles of practice. In the last analysis, the theoretical employment of reasons presupposes the practical employment of reason and the practical up-shot of pragmatic contradiction is that not all things are permitted. The foundations of the sense of obligation without which responsibility has little meaning rest upon this self-referential aspect of practice. An historical account of this notion of self-reference is given, starting with Plato's definition of knowledge in the *Theaetetus* and Socrates' disclaimer of wisdom in the *Apology*, then on through Augustine to Descartes' *Cogito*, its most famous example. Treating this argument from our point of view, the ideal of self-reference is expanded and exemplified and the force of the enabling conditions applied in the context of practice. The normativeness of the enabling conditions is recognized through reflection and grounded in self-reference and it comes with the recognition of my necessary inclusion as a person under the class-conditions, as so far enumerated, of purposive activity. Reflective beings can discover the moral grounded in their own experience in the sense that neglect of it destroys the human capacity. Yet, in so far as they act in the light of this discovery in the many ways and varying facets of their practice, they create and sustain something that would not be, otherwise, and in so doing they create and sustain themselves as free and responsible persons. This capacity, as Kant saw better than many, is the ground for the individual as ultimate value. The result is social as well as individual.

Nothing is categorically binding from the theoretical standpoint, but, if we step inside the context of practice, where we always are, then the enabling conditions take on their categorically normative function as moral "oughts."

Chapter Nine, Corporate Character, concerns the application of moral responsibility to the corporation. It is claimed that moral judgments of activity cannot be made on corporations. But along with judgments of activity, we make moral judgments of character and the relationship between character and action, first in persons and then in corporations, is examined. The connection between character and action in individuals is missing in the case of the corporation and, since character shepherds action, we conclude that corporate character is the responsibility of management and that judgments of "good" or "bad" character with respect to corporations are morally meaningful.

In Conclusion, Chapter Ten, tries to restate the point of view advanced in these chapters and considers some of the implications of making practice fundamental. Much will be said that would lead directly to a metaphysics of practice, but that is beyond the present purpose.

Footnote

1. *Ethics and Profits: The Crisis in Confidence in American Business*, New York: Simon and Schuster, 1976, p. 128-9. Hereafter, E&P.

Introduction

CHAPTER 1

The aim of this book is to consider the moral foundations of business practice. I do not mean to imply by this that there is a separate ethics or moral theory for business as opposed to any other kind of practice, i.e., medicine or carpentry. On the contrary, it is a moral theory of practice as such that is to be advanced here, one that is applicable to all practice including business. But business practice will be the context of our discussion, rather than practice itself, because that is what I am interested in and because from this perspective several things can be said about practice in general as well as about business practice in particular which are not often said and should be.

Within this broader context of business practice the question of the foundations of moral responsibility is most complex for a number of reasons. First, a bridge connecting the hitherto separate enterprises of business and philosophical ethics must be built, for, while many people talk about business and morality in the same breath, it is far from clear in most cases what the inherent connection between the two may be. In fact, a rather large portion of received opinion on the matter seems to be that there is no such connection at all; you take off your hat, your coat and your morals when you enter your place of business. It is the theory of practice just alluded to above that will perform this function. Secondly, we must set out the appropriate grounds for judgments of individual moral responsibility and, since most business practice in the Western World falls within a corporate context, determine whether and to what extent such grounds are applicable to corporations themselves as well as to managers. Hopefully, this will be accomplished as a result of considering our description of practice and its conditions from the point of view of practice itself. And lastly, it is a complex question because within this broadest framework, business practice, at least three levels can be distinguished and to each of these levels important elements of the nature and meaning of moral responsibility in business practice can be traced. These levels will be set forth now, and then, our procedure in what is to follow with respect to them will be described.

At the first level there are the activities and practices which we recognize as belonging to corporations themselves—"U.S. Steel raises its prices 4.3%" or "The United Automobile Workers and Chrysler are negotiating a new contract" or "The Metropolitan Opera broadcasts are sponsored by Texaco." Even though the courts consider corporations to be persons with certain legal rights and obligations it is obvious that this way of speaking cloaks a "legal fiction" and that in some very important ways corporate entities are not like persons at all. Certainly, however, the notion of the corporation as a person is not a complete fiction and it is not inappropriate, as we go along, to look out for those aspects of this "corporate fiction" that allow it to function as successfully as it in fact does.

Yet a second level of this business context shows up as a remedy for one of the defects of the corporate fiction, the fact that corporate entities cannot initiate or carry on action on their own. Natural persons are required to act as agents for corporations and this is where the level of management appears. Even within the most autocratic managerial hierarchy where you do as you are told, a manager is, nonetheless, expected to do it responsibly and is held accountable if he does not. Corporations need responsible agents. How such managers exercise this agency may well be determined by the needs of the corporation as interpreted by the top brass. But the capacity to act responsibly which managers hopefully possess, points up the third level of the business context, the level of natural persons, as such, where the capacity to be responsible originates. Being a manager is just one of the activities natural persons can engage in and the activities of natural persons functioning as managers permeate the corporate context. We have then the corporate, the managerial and the personal levels to consider and it should be clear that they are not just separate parts of the corporate context for they fold in on one another. What we have are a number of natural persons who in their capacity as managers are acting as agents for the corporation. But treating them as distinct levels will be useful in trying to discover in what sense the notion of responsibility can be justly applied to the first level distinguished, the corporation, and in what sense it cannot be. I believe this to be the best way to show the relationship of ethics to the activities of business and management and the idea of obligation will be central.

Without any doubt at all, corporate structure is the most pervasive form of organization in our society. It has been the engine of our growth and development over the last hundred and fifty years. It has been given special recognition as being central to our progress as a people and as an inducement to more of the same. And it has been filling up the social space between the individual and the nation-state (and beyond) by leaps and bounds. Even governmental structure itself at all levels is perhaps best understood in the same terms, as a variant on general corporate structure. But setting aside the sense in which government on the federal, state and local levels is corporate, my concern here lies with the huge number of public corporations which are, again, past doubting, by far the most powerful elements in our society.

The problem can be expressed in several ways. One way is to observe that the modern corporation came into being as an extension of the power and flexibility of the individual, as part and parcel of the modern concern with individual freedom and development. It has filled the structural gap left by the break-up of feudalism and its very success has given it such dominion and power over us all that regulation by the community at large has come about. Because the power to regulate is the power to destroy as well as to stimulate, the question of the most adequate way to regulate corporate activity arises. Any sensible answer to this question presupposes an answer to a prior question concerning what it is you want your regulation to accomplish. In the United States we are now in the midst of having second thoughts about this prior question.

Another way to put the problem is to point out that much is being said about the responsibilities of the corporate community to everybody and everything, starting at the traditional center with duties to stockholders, radiating outward through those to consumers and the general community and coming to rest on corporate responsibility to the total environment including the support systems for the biosphere. But all the while very little that is helpful is being said about the foundations of all this responsibility. Why should corporations be responsible? What is usually given in reply is a litany of the duties of business and the attitudes of managers that rests either on some assumed sort of "self-interest," which becomes more "enlightened" as it reaches beyond narrow, selfish concerns, or on the fact of community pressure. The appeal to self-interest might work very well if in fact my interests fall somewhere along this range of increasing enlightenment, but it says precious little about why I "ought" to be interested at all. Most self-interest theories do not bother to justify self-interest. Instead, they merely assume that everyone is self-interested, which may in fact be true but is beside the point as an explanation of why I "ought" to be self-interested. In clarification of this point, Professor Clark writes:

> But the concept (enlightened self-interest) is misused whenever it is carried to the point of claiming that it does away with the need for genuinely ethical standards. This means treating others as mere means to the ends of self; and this is contrary to the basic ethics of a free and humane society....[1]

On the other hand, the appeal to community pressure is straight power talk of the "might makes right" variety and provides no basis for the determination of which pressures should be bowed to and which should be resisted and to what extent. Both of these attempts to ground responsibility deprive such talk of any sense of obligation, in fact of any moral nub at all. At the very least, this makes one wonder just how the notion of responsibility is being used. Someone might suggest that the difficult problems of responsibility and obligation can be avoided if we use the notion of accountability; corporations need only be accountable to their stockholders or the community at large. But it is not clear how anyone can be accountable to anyone else for something he is not responsible for. I cannot be held accountable to anyone for my blue eyes. But as a citizen I can be held accountable for the actions for which I am responsible. It is very clear that there are all kinds of group and social pressures to which we are subjected and if we would uphold the value of the individual some answer other than social pressure must be found. In the last analysis to provide such an answer is the over-riding reason for advancing a brand of rationalism here and such objectivity is as important as a basis for individual moral decision as it is for scientific method. For, in its absence, fifty million Frenchmen can't be wrong and there is no hope for the settlement of differences other than the power of the club.

Yet another way of writing about these matters, now much in use, is the ideological approach. Corporate activity is found to be an expression or function of a certain set of beliefs or values during a certain period of history. Now, under changing conditions, this set of beliefs and values is being modified to handle the new circumstances. The old ideology is no longer adequate and the wave of the future is the new set shaping up. The implication is that anyone who is not an antiquarian will point his nose in the direction of the future. There is much to be learned from this kind of developmental analysis and comparison provided that somewhere along the way questions of truth and obligation are treated. But in the total absence of such considerations, this approach reads like a fashion report.

There are even some pious references to the moral, now and again, accompanied by the use of moral language (the use of "responsibility" in phrases like "social responsibility" is a case in point), but until and unless some attempt is made to ground obligation, to step the moral mast, so to speak, the whole concern with corporate responsibility is at the mercy of the winds. Philosophical ethics might have been expected to remedy this, but hasn't done much except confirm the vagaries of wind and current during the last generation. Having shown to its satisfaction that the "ought" cannot be grounded on the "is," it appears that the moral enterprise is adrift.

Perhaps the most general and historically interesting way of approaching this whole problem is reflected in Professor James Coleman's book, *Power and the Structure of Society*, when he tells us "if you want to know what is new in the modern world, it is the modern corporation."[2] Quite clearly, our question about the foundations of responsibility in business practice presupposes yet another question: How are we to understand this new phenomenon?

In general, the answer to this question put forward in these pages is that corporate activity can best be understood on analogy with the activity of persons. Even though our concern will not be directly with the analogy itself, nevertheless our analysis of activity as the basis for responsibility will of necessity be modeled on the activity of persons. I want to consider what I take to be several good reasons for taking this analogy seriously.

The first of these reasons is historical and based upon the fact that the legal conception of the corporation was fashioned after the legal conception of a natural person. Considering the historical growth of the corporate idea, Abraham Chayes writes,

> To fit the corporation for American service, the first task was to strip away

> communal overtones, the garments of special privilege and restrictionism that still clung to it. Corporate organization was to be transmuted from the boon of a whimsical sovereign into a right which was to be readily available to all. The corporation was changed from a body politic into a persona ficta. As a legal person it was qualified to bear all the rights with which an age of individualism generously clothed persons of flesh and blood.[3]

The term "fiction" has a sense of the false or unreal about it for us, perhaps, but in this usage it refers to something created by man without counterpart in the natural order, hence, an artificial person as over against the idea of the natural person which does have a referent in the nature of things. Such corporate persons are understood as initiating and carrying out activities as people do and the limits of their activities are laid down in terms of rights, privileges, and obligations much as it is with natural persons. As example, and an historically important one in the growth of the corporate idea, consider the opinion of the Supreme Court in the Allgeyer Case where the interpretation of the 14th Amendment is applied to persons in general including the corporation:

> The liberty mentioned in that Amendment means not only the right of the citizen to be free from physical restraint of his person, but the term is deemed to embrace the right of the citizen to be free in the enjoyment of all his faculties; to be free to use them in all lawful ways, to live and work where he will; to earn his livelihood by any lawful calling; to pursue any livelihood or avocation; and for that purpose to enter into all contracts which may be proper, necessary, and essential to his carrying out to a successful conclusion the purposes above mentioned...[4]

It is the due process clause of that Amendment which has served as the primary protection of private enterprise since the Civil War.[5] The fact that the legal idea of the corporation developed historically along these lines argues at least for the initial plausibility of the suggested analogy with persons.

A second reason is that while the corporation may have rights and powers as well as duties, these cannot be exercised except by persons acting as corporate agents. This instrumental function of persons within the corporation framework includes not only management but employees as well. In fact, by extension, two other types of persons can be included as affecting corporate activity, the investor and the consumer. In speaking of the "active wealth" of corporate management, Berle and Means point out that:

> the group in control of a large modern corporation is astride an organism which has little real value except as it continues to function (and)...is dependent for (its life) on its security holders, ...workers and consumers, but most of all (its) mainspring, ...'control.'[6]

Corporate activity is surrounded by, shot through with and totally dependent upon the activities of persons and this leads to another, and perhaps the best, reason for thinking of corporate activity on analogy with persons.

Originally, corporations were the instruments of the people who formed them but, in their modern development, it is the people who have become the instruments of corporate purpose; the tail began to wag the dog. The result has been a widespread loss of freedom by persons. But equally as important is the loss of power—the sense of being reduced to something less than a person should be, or even, used to be. The classic example is the consumer with a just complaint looking for satisfaction. Locating someone with responsibility is no easy job. There are exceptions, but very often you get nowhere unless you are willing to make a career of your complaint and a long term investment of time. The only real defense against being completely reduced is to consider corporations to be like persons and to hold them responsible to ourselves and society in the same way that persons are held responsible to each other and to society in general. Nothing will dehumanize our society more completely than to have the most powerful elements in that society treated and thought about in non-human ways. When I first began to study Philosophy I remember reading that anthropomorphism, the attribution of human characteristics to non-human things or beings, was unscientific and wrong. This complaint is at least as old as Zenophanes who, about 510 B.C., vilified Homer for writing about the gods in the same way. And it must be admitted there is some "right reason" in the complaint although not sufficient to spoil my appreciation of Disney's animal cartoons. Nonetheless, there are limits and where human creations such as society and its institutions are concerned, a certain bedrock anthropomorphism is positive virtue, in the absence of which, for humans, "nothing beside remains."

There is yet a further reason for taking the proposed analogy seriously in the way we talk about corporations and their activities (the aforementioned phrase "corporate responsibility" is again a case in point). So far as I know no one tries to show that any kind of finite being other than humans can be responsible and even that is roundly debated every so often. To attribute responsibility to corporations suggests the proposed analogy, whether correctly or incorrectly.

Lastly, this way of talking is common in the law. Consider, as example, the wording in the Sherman Anti-Trust Act of 1890:

> Every person who shall monopolize, or attempt to monopolize, or combine or conspire with any other person or persons to monopolize any part of the trade or commerce among the several states, or with foreign nations, shall be guilty of a misdemeanor...

It might be objected here that the reference to "persons" in the Act points up the fact that it was John D. Rockefeller and not Standard Oil per se that was the problem. But, while this may have been true in some particular cases, the term "person" covers both at law and that is the point to be noted. Only persons can "conspire", "combine" or even "be guilty."

Prior to the historic study in 1934 by Berle and Means, quoted from previously (p. 5), it was assumed that corporations were instruments of their owners and would operate within the purposes for which their owners formed them. As long as this instrumental relationship obtained the locus of responsibility for corporate action was simply assignable to the owners. But as the separation of ownership (stockholders) and control (management) develops, this traditional locus of corporate responsibility evaporates. The result has been likened to a corporate Frankenstein monster having all the power of pooled resources, the ability to perpetuate that power and no responsibility beyond what the law requires. It is in just this way that the legitimacy of corporate power is brought into question today, for the prospects for the misuse of such power are at least as frightening for ordinary mortals as they were in the older and less sophisticated era of the "robber barons." As example, consider the effects of the recent "mistake" by the management of the automobile industry with respect to small, fuel-efficient cars. The economic reverberations of that mis-judgment involved the jobs and support structures for 350,000 persons. There are those who in the face of threats of such magnitude see nothing but a tight-fisted set of laws and regulations for the protection of the public. And of course much of the regulation that has come about through the years has been in response to just such perils. A closer look at the separation of ownership and control is needed.

Berle and Means point out that when the split comes about the purposes of the managers need no longer be those of the owners.[7] There is a general agreement that corporate objectives in the post-World War II era-have been "survival, growth, profit, economic contribution and social obligations" in that order.[8]

Consider also the statement by the Committee for Economic Development:

> As a permanent institution, the large corporation is developing long-term goals such as survival, growth, and increasing respect and acceptance by the public. Current profitability, once regarded as the dominant if not exclusive objective, is now often seen more as a vital means and powerful motivating force for achieving broader ends, rather than as an end in itself.[9]

Prior to the split, corporate goals were presumably those of the owners. But with the split something striking comes about which is implicit in the objectives of survival and growth and indicative of an important state in the development of the corporate idea; with the advent of the split, the corporation becomes an end-in-itself with its own objectives. Of course, in the last analysis it is not possible for the character of anything i.e., the corporation, to be wholly instrumental. Even something such as a can opener, whose very name indicates its predominantly instrumental nature, cannot be wholly an instrument for there are certain conditions or characteristics which must be present in the can opener by virtue of which it will be able to fulfill its instrumental function of opening cans. Those conditions constitute the in-itselfness of the can opener as an entity and are the enabling conditions of its instrumental function. As Aristotle would have put it—act is prior to potency—or instrumentality is a dependent form of being. It is this condition which is being noted when someone who has created an instrument, either a thing or an organization, to carry out a determinate function, discovers that his creation has a life of its own.[10] Selfstanding individuality is an enabling condition of self-interest and with the recognition of the split between owners and management, the American corporation has become a thing-in-itself whose well-being may be the aim of its practice and, it should be noted without malice, a fit instrument for the self-interest of its managers.

Management acquires a vested interest in the survival of the corporation it controls and the giving of an adequate return on investment to the owners becomes just one of the conditions of survival. And since nothing stands still, growth is also a condition of survival as well as of increased power for management. And so management becomes a profession instead of an appendage. As end-in-itself, corporate activity aims first at satisfying those demands which must be met to maintain itself.

Previously, in mentioning the results of the split, it was noted that its occurrence removed the traditional grounds of responsibility, the owners, from the picture leaving a monster on the loose. That is partly true, but there is more to the story. For, when the split made the corporation an end-in-itself, apart from the ends of the owners, it created the basic condition without which there can be no responsibility whatsoever; the corporation becomes something in its own right. Prior to that point, the courts' treatment of corporations as persons was an acknowledged fiction. Since then, the basic building block of responsible activity, self-standing individuality, has been present. Or put in another way, the courts have developed the idea of the corporation on analogy with the person for several hundred years and in large part this development has occurred in our country over the last one hundred and seventy-five years. As long ago as 1819 in *Dartmouth College vs. Woodward*, Chief Justice Marshall, referring to the "artificial being" of the corporation, wrote of the properties of such being:

> Among the most important are immortality, and if the expression may be allowed, individuality; properties by which a perpetual succession of many persons are considered as the same, and may act as a single individual. They enable a corporation to manage its own affairs....[11]

But it wasn't until the split between ownership and control was recognized that the independent status which is a precondition of personhood came into existence. The parallel between the corporation and the nation-state in the light of this is compelling and the corporation has been characterized, especially in its multinational form, as being like a nation-state in its independence. The parallel between the corporation and the natural person in these respects is also compelling and the corporation can be characterized, especially in its modern form, as being like a person in its independence. And the question is how do we bring about the responsible exercise of this independence?

The problem of the legitimacy of corporate power raised by the separation of ownership and control is not a new problem. Rather, it is a species of a very familiar problem in the modern world. In the so-called Modern Period in Western European Civilization, it is almost a truism to say that the basic interest has been with the individuality of man. This, of course, translates directly into the importance of freedom and is expressed in the Protestant Reformation as well as the political theory of the state. The difficulty has been to square authority and obligation with the fact of freedom so as not to undercut the independence and integrity of the individual.

This is not easy to do as a moments reflection will show. The most notable example of squaring authority and freedom in human experience occurs in rational persuasion; A explains something to B and B accepts A's explanation, not because it is A's but because it "makes sense" or "is reasonable." The point being that B makes the explanation his own in his understanding of it as reasonable even though it comes from a source other than himself. The conditions favoring this non-violent persuasion are, in one sense, all too seldom encountered and yet, in another, they undergird by far the largest part of our daily commerce in the world.

Of all the theories of political and social organization put forward in the last four hundred years to square authority and freedom only that of Immanuel Kant sets out to locate the source of authority and obligation within the individual himself. To go in this direction means the individual is ultimate in ways which bear, I believe, very heavily upon our problem of moral responsibility and the value of the analogy between corporations and persons suggested herein. Near the beginning of his celebrated article in the New York Times Magazine (12 Sept. 1970), "The Social Responsibility of Business Is to Increase Its Profits," Milton Friedman, in his critique of the whole notion of "social responsibility" as applicable to business, writes:

> The discussions of the "social responsibilities of business" are notable for their analytical looseness and lack of rigor. What does it mean to say that "business" has responsibilities? Only people can have responsibilities. A corporation is an artificial person and in this sense may have artificial responsibilities, but "business" as a whole cannot be said to have responsibilities, even in this vague sense.

The passage quoted above is no model of analytical precision and rigor itself for we can certainly refer to "business" or the "business community" in the aggregate and say that it has responsibilities, for instance, to the law, by which we mean that any and all businesses have a responsibility to obey any and all laws which pertain to their operations. Certainly, there can be no quarrel with that usage. And the usage of "social responsibility" in its application to "business" is exactly parallel and need not be taken for anything more. It is true, I submit, that, as Friedman says, "only people can have responsibilities" and the implication of the sentence following is that corporations, at best, are only artificial persons not real ones and that their responsibilities at best are only artificial and not real ones. Just what an artificial responsibility could be is anything but clear. Corporate responsibility for existing laws couldn't be called an artificial responsibility, could it? It would appear that while the corporation is an artificial person in the sense that it is created by the law, the responsibilities which this artificial person has to the law, to its employees, stockholders and customers are anything but artificial. By the same token I may have an artificial leg but there is nothing artificial about the walking I do with it. To imply that such is the case in either instance is loose, vague and misinforming usage in the extreme. This point is a small one and of little moment except that it points to the question "What are we talking about when we say that some person has a responsibility?" With persons this seems to mean that certain behavior is expected of them;

with respect to the law, we expect them to obey it. We also talk about persons being responsible and here we are speaking of a quality of their behavior. Is it wrong or nonsense to talk about a corporation as having a responsibility or being responsible in the same sense? Are there any grounds for supposing the behavior of corporations to be similar enough to that of persons to justify application of the idea of responsibility in either sense to them? Clearly, it is the activity of persons that is responsible or otherwise and it is the activity of corporations that is considered at law to be responsible or otherwise. There is no other grip which law can exercise on persons and corporations than through their activities. It isn't a matter of how they are constituted, whether, like persons, they come into being by legislative act or, as in some European countries, by custom. It is a matter of the nature of the activities they engage in. As we shall see there is ample warrant for treating their activities similarly to the way we treat the activities of persons; in fact, there is no other way to treat them.

In defense of this analogy between persons and corporations let me make reference to the prizewinning and insightful book of Professor Alfred D. Chandler, Jr., *The Visible Hand: The Managerial Revolution in American Business,* where, in explicating the first of eight propositions which the book as a whole demonstrates concerning the development of the visible hand of management, he says:

> This proposition is derived directly from the definition of a modern business enterprise. Such an enterprise came into being and continued to grow by setting up or purchasing business units that were theoretically able to operate as independent enterprises - in other words, by internalizing the activities that had been or could be carried on by several business units and the transactions that had been or could be carried on between them.[12]

The use of the word "internalizing" to describe the organizing of what were separate actions previously into one continuous, controlled activity is wonderfully and appropriately suggestive. The Freudian psychologist uses this term to describe the process by which the moral norms of a society become the Super-Ego, the conscience of the individual. It is also the term used to render what the teachings of Jesus are usually given credit for doing to the law of the Hebrews - internalizing it. Instead of externally observed ritual action on designated sites and occasions, the law became a set of principles applied and lived in the light of by the believer. This same internalization is found in Second Isaiah and the teachings of Hillel, but no matter the source, and one could argue that the message of the existing, so-called civilized religions in the world today arose as externalized ritual behavior became unsatisfactory for handling problems of *meum* and *teum* and an internalization in terms of principle began to take its place. Should my appeal to the religious to clarify bother anyone, consider a life lived in the meeting and fulfilling of external demands or even the changing quality of your own feelings as opposed to a life lived according to and in the light of a fund of principle. How might you characterize the latter in relation to the former? Internalization is not an inappropriate way to characterize what we shall later on call the control dimension of practice, and Chandler's choice of the term to characterize what management does when it interrelates, coordinates, controls and plans for, with speed and efficiency, the various elements that make up corporate activity is very apt. All principled behavior exhibits this characteristic, internalization, and while, by itself, it does not involve excessive power, behaving in such fashion is a source of power. When coupled with what Chandler calls the conditions of high volume in production and distribution, the railroad and the telegraph, the growth in power in corporate America beggars the imagination. In the same fashion, it is hoped the analogy between the activities of persons and corporations will generate power in understanding.

Now, by way of summary and pointing ahead, it has been suggested that we can better understand the corporation and its responsibilities if we think of it as being like an individual person in certain respects. The foundation for this analogy can be made clearer if we further suggest that the key to responsibility in persons lies in the activities they engage in and one of the things that persons and corporations have in common is that both engage in activity. It must be remembered throughout these remarks that an analogy involves a similarity and not an identity; by no stretch of the imagination am I saying that a corporation is a person. Analogies have their limitations and a grasp of those limitations is partly constitutive of a reasoned application and appreciation of the analogy itself.

The nature of activity will be crucial throughout because persons are responsible for their activities and, similarly, it is in the activity of corporations that we look for and demand the exercise of responsibility.

In essence we shall attempt to lay out the groundwork for a personal, social and corporate ethics by spelling out the conditions of responsible activity by an agent. As will be seen, these conditions must be developed and maintained, and can be destroyed by individuals and by corporate structures including government. Such conditions lay out the idea for practice and constitute the only real safety and security as well as the only real freedom and opportunity for anyone. Without them, anything goes, our civilization is a sham and these remarks nonsense. The argument will be that the sense in which this analysis of activity in persons can be sensibly applied to all three levels of business practice is the only sense in which any of the three levels, including the corporate, can be meaningfully spoken of as morally responsible. And, if successful, the sense in which moral responsibility is applicable to business practice in our society will be clearer then it is at present.

Footnotes

1. Clark, John Maurice, *The Ethical Basis of Economic Freedom*, The Kazanjian Foundation Lectures, Westport, CT: The Calvin K. Kazanjian Economics Foundation, 1955, p. 33.

2. New York: W. W. Norton, 1974, p. 14

3. Quoted by John R. Davis in *Corporations*, Capricorn Books: New York, 1961, p. v.

4. Allgeyer v. Louisiana, 165 U.S. 578, 589 (1897)

5. Cf. Bernard Schwartz, *The Reins of Power: A Constitutional History of the United States*, American Century Series, New York: Hill and Wang, 1963, p. 122

6. Berle, Adolf A., Jr. and Gardner C. Means, *The Modern Corporation and Private Property*, New York: The Macmillan Company, 1934, p. 348

7. Ibid., p. 121ff

8. Luthans and Hodgetts, p. 38

9. *Social Responsibilities of Business Corporations*, New York, 1971, p. 22

10. cf. Dukas' *The Sorcerer's Apprentice*

11. 17 U.S. (4. Weat.) 518 (1819).

12. Cambridge, Massachusetts: The Belknap Press of Harvard University Press, 1977 p. 6

Practice and Its Presuppositions

CHAPTER 2

The Elements of Practice

If what persons and corporations have in common is "activity," then what is needed is an analysis spelling out its nature and characteristics allowing us to distinguish those elements common to all practice with special application to business practice. Hopefully, upon those elements a theory of moral responsibility can be grounded, one that will be applicable to all levels of activity. I shall begin by making use of a description of activity developed by Albury Castell in *The Self in Philosophy.* [1] In that work Professor Castell sets forth the differences between "process" and "activity" and in the analysis to follow my aim is a faithful rendition of the elements of activity as found in Castell. It will be in some detail in order to establish this context of human practice as underlying all of the ideas in this work. Following this exposition, two implications drawn by Castell will be considered because of their importance for the argument later on, as well as one implication of our own concerning the bi-polar nature of practice. Then, although all of the characteristics of practice will be seen to cluster around one or both of these poles, it is being "presuppositioned" or "having presuppositions" which will occupy our attention for the remainder of the chapter.

Castell begins by considering astronomy, the science that studies the nature and movements of the solar system. The movements of the planets within this system are examples of process. Astronomizing, on the other hand, is the discipline that studies the nature and movements of the solar system. This discipline is an example of activity.[2] It is in contrasting the science of astronomy with the discipline of astronomizing that Castell develops the distinction between "process" and "activity."[3] A parallel distinction can be made in the field of economics between the system of economic theory and the discipline of economics which not only discovers and formulates economic theories but practices in the light of those theories either well or poorly. In the same way business is basically a discipline, a practice making use of the body of theory and principle relevant to its nature as an activity. In my exposition of Castell's characteristics of activity, needed examples and illustration will come from business practice as our primary concern, but it will be clear that they apply to all practice as such. It should also be clear that the order of their presentation is not significant in itself. For the most part, it is that of Castell.

1. Business practice is *fallible,* mistakes can be made, practices can fail as well as succeed.

2. Business practice is *purposive,* a goal is being sought, an end aimed at, it is teleological; in the case of business, serving the customer, creating a product, making a profit or running the business. Here it must be noted, there is an implicit duality in "purposive" that needs to be made explicit because of its importance for our understanding of activity. Not only does "purposive" involve *a goal* but it also involves *aiming at* that goal. There is a bi-polarity here, that will be referred to as the goal pole and the control pole and will become the basis for the two dimensions of practice.

3. Business practice is *experimental* and tentative (this is related to fallibility). Knowing what you want doesn't ensure success. The proper method is required and experimentation is called for.

4. Business practice is *critical,* that is, it is carried out with reference to criteria. It is guided by specifiable values; it is not value free but guided by norms. The principles of supply and demand may be value free but their application in practice is not.

5. Business practice is *reasoned,* subject to justification. This is not the same as purpose. To give a reason is to justify. For example, suppose you are in St. Louis, want to go to Chicago and decide to go south to get there. I might ask "Why are you going south?" You might reply, "The earth is round and I am in no hurry," as justification, which is related to but not the same as purpose. You are giving me reasons for your unusual choice of means to achieve your end. Going north would be the fastest, most direct and usual means for getting to Chicago from St. Louis.

6. Business practice is a *locus for choice* between alternatives. Where there is no choice there is no practice or activity. In so far as success is a function of management it depends upon right choice and failure upon wrong choice.

7. Business practice is the *locus for responsibility,* sound management is responsible management. Sometimes, in response to present conditions one does things that would never be chosen if one had more room and the lack of alternatives tends to mitigate responsibility. Of course, that in itself tends to qualify as irresponsible management. Neither, it seems, is ignorance an excuse; one is hired to be responsible. How far such responsibility extends is another question.

8. Business practice is *corrigible,* error can be detected and corrected. It has always been one of the recognized beauties of the scientific method that it is self-correcting and this quality is found in all practice that is responsible.

9. Business practice is *meaningful.* It is difficult to say what constitutes meaning

or without what, meaning would be absent, but without meaning practice would be impossible. A good manager knows what he is doing, that is, his activity is meaningful. Present alternatives have meaning in relation to his purposes. But something can be said about meaning—giving meaning to meaning—without fear of error. Meaning arises only as an object or event is related to something other than itself and in a special way. Neither the object "chair" nor the word "chair" has any meaning by itself. But the concept "chair" has meaning because it embodies two levels of reference related in hierarchical fashion. The best illustration is a definition; "chair" means a piece of furniture (its genus) to sit on (its specific differentia)—what distinguishes this type of furniture from all other types, i.e., "bed," "table," "bureau," etc.

10. Business practice is *judgmental,* one makes judgments constantly in business and hopefully, they are consistent, well-founded and successful.

11. Business practice has *presuppositions*—anyone practicing will come to realize that certain conditions must be present for it to take place. Without them, no practice.

12. Business practice requires the distinction between the *ideal and the real.* Errors occur and ideally they should not. Practice must recognize the difference between what is and what ought to be.

13. Business practice is *educable,* that is, error can be reduced and technique perfected.

14. Business practice has *no spatial dimension or direction* necessarily connected with it. It may very well involve motion in space but it does not have to.

15. Business practice involves *response to a challenge*. Response to a stimulus is automatic; response to a challenge is deliberate and critical.

A moment's reflection on these fifteen characteristics of practice will show them to be interrelated; some, in fact, are dependent upon others. While all are important in revealing the differing aspects of practice, some mark out the outlines more clearly than others. The meanings of "fallible" (1), "experimental" (3), "corrigible" (8), and "educable" (13), seem to involve and illuminate one another as do "critical" (4), "reasoned" (5), "meaningful" (9), "judgmental" (10), and "the distinction between real and ideal" (12). And these two groups, coupled with "locus of choice" (6), explain what is meant by "locus of responsibility" (7). "Choice" and "responsibility" indicate what is meant by "presuppositions" (11); without freedom of choice and the capacity to initiate action, activity would be impossible. In a general sense, "purposive" (2) is the most fundamental of all, and it is essential to bear in mind that "purposive," as applied to activity, implies the other characteristics enumerated and not merely the goal-directed processes of guided missiles, calculators, and other systems with built-in ends. "Purposive" also describes what might be called the transcending function of activity which leads beyond itself and is quite appropriate for a creature of limited means with needs and interests reaching beyond those limits. Coupled with "response to a challenge" (15), "purposive" conveys the sense of activity as being grounded *in medias res* and responsive to that content rather than simply a spinning out from within. There are other ways to relate these characteristics but "purposive" appears descriptively most fundamental and indicates the bi-polar nature of activity; one focus on the goal or end and the other focus on initiating, guiding and maintaining the conditions of activity itself. Most of the characteristics we have been talking about illuminate the focus of control, this inner dimension. But altogether these characteristics are descriptive of the bi-polar shape of this purposiveness.

Perhaps it would be helpful to imagine practice as an arrow of intent or force with its source and center at one end and the arrow-head of its purpose and reach at the other.

Before moving on to consider in detail the characteristic "having presuppositions," there are two further points about activity, made by Castell, that are important to see. When you reflect upon it, it appears true beyond doubt that there are activities as described above for the simple reason that the denial that there are activities is itself an activity having the characteristics set forth above.[4] It should be noted, however, that this does not constitute a proof of activity, but it does cut the ground from under the opposition in the same way the skeptic is silenced (what C.I. Lewis called a "pragmatic contradiction"[5]). The skeptic wishes to deny there is any knowledge, but in so doing, his denial, "There is no knowledge," counts as what? He may remain silent, but he cannot assert or practice his belief without self-refutation. The denial of activity faces the same fate. We shall return to this self-referential type of argument later on as a central consideration of practice, as primary in the search for a foundation for responsibility and the moral "ought." But with regard to the reality of activity a difficult question arises: Does the fact of activity imply an agent carrying it out?[6] For example, if activity is purposive, aims at some end, then there must be something continuous and identical throughout the span of activity to direct it, an agent or self. Such a continuous and identical self is a sine qua non of practice. But if I am free to accept the reality of practice having the characteristics set forth above, because to deny its reality asserts it, then I must also accept the enabling conditions of practice, those conditions without which practice could not come about. In what follows then, we shall suppose that activity presupposes a "self," but shall mean by "self" no more than the continuity and identity with itself required to make activity possible. As the elements of activity become clearer we may very well have to modify this limited idea of self, but until we can see the reasons for so doing let us be parsimonious with the conception of "self" or "agency" involved.

The Presuppositions of Practice

Ethics has to do with the principles of conduct and practice and we want to find out if there are any principles of practice, of activity, as we have described it.

We can begin by considering one of the characteristics of activity more closely — activity has "presuppositions" (11). In the broadest sense, the presuppositions of an event are the conditions in the absence of which the event could not come about.

As example, consider the activity of baking a cake, planning a trip or writing this sentence: unless certain conditions are fulfilled, conditions arising out of the nature of baking, planning, and writing, these activities are impossible to carry out. Our present concern with ecology is for the conditions of life—conditions without which life could not be. Or more generally, consider the so-called three laws of thought, Identity (A is A), Excluded Middle (either A or not A) and Non-Contradiction (not both A and not A). If you reflect upon the activity of thinking you will see that there can be no thinking —dream or phantasy, perhaps—but no thinking unless these three laws are adhered to. Thinking presupposes them. It is not as informative to say that these laws are true for all thought, perhaps, as to say that these laws are normative for all thinking. C.I. Lewis observed that they constitute the "morality of thought."[7] Our question becomes "Are there any conditions without which activity or practice is impossible?" Or, "What are the enabling conditions of practice?"

It was pointed out that purposive activity is bi-polar and there are two sets of necessary conditions involved, those pertaining to the "self-pole" exercising initiation and control and those pertaining to the end aimed at, or world in which practice takes place. We have seen that freedom of choice is a presupposition of purposive activity. For me to be able to do what I am doing in writing this sentence, it is necessary that I be free to choose. Notice again, this is not a proof of freedom; there can be none. But it does mean that as far as my purposive activity or practice is concerned, I must consider myself as free with respect to it. However, such freedom would mean nothing unless there were real alternatives, the world or context in which activity takes place must contain real "multiplicity." Freedom as the ability to choose and to initiate appropriate action requires not only that there exist real alternatives in the outside world — you cannot make someone act responsibly, but you can give or take away the conditions permitting them to do so — but, also, that there are real alternatives in your inside world as well; a certain relation to the past is required, one in which the various events of the past are items in the present of the chooser, i.e., my having studied languages in the past and my ability to employ them as the situations in which I find myself require them. In fact, only to the extent that the above condition is met could one be said to have a past that has really "passed." It is doubtful if a completely determined creature could even have a past. Some kind of epiphenomenal awareness perhaps, but only of what is, not of what was, not of a past as passed. At the very least, purposive activity requires a measure of detachment from previous history, of independence in the choice and initiation of action. To be aware of your own history, you cannot be completely embedded in it. The double aspect of consciousness, being aware you are aware, affords the possibility of such detachment as well as of aiming at a goal. Further, purposive practice would not be possible without the application of continuous effort and in a world of discontinuous, atomistic states the perdurance of directed effort would not be possible. If there is no continuity between a choice and its consequent, its result, then there is nothing more than the constant conjunction of discontinuous states in the external world. The thrust of activity cannot be understood at all as discontinuous states. The whole push of purpose is lost. Inner "concern" and outer "continuity," then, are the second pair of presuppositions, if practice is to be possible.

There is one other condition belonging to the control pole of activity, that of "consistency." Practice requires choice in a stable and connected manner, not of a willy-nilly sort and not in such a way as to cut the ground out from under either itself, the sought for goal, or previous actions taken in pursuit of it. The three norms of thinking spoken of recently are expressions of this presupposition. Its correlate in the outer world is "structure" — unless there is order, that is, stable connection between elements and states of the world, no goal could ever be attained nor could you go about getting somewhere from anywhere else. Only so can choice be efficacious.

Applying "consistency" in the form of the laws of thinking to the control pole of practice as a requisite for intelligibility would bother no one, but that these same norms should be inherent also in the presupposition of structure pertaining to the outer world may seem bothersome. On the face of it, to deny that there is an external world and that, even though we can make mistakes, we do know a good deal about its order and structure would be totally unwarranted. But it is also unwarranted to assume there is some final structure out there as the only condition enabling knowledge. At the close of *Mind and the World Order*, C.I. Lewis makes a point important for us here when he writes:

> The mind will always be capable of discovering that order which is requisite to knowledge, because a mind such as ours, set down in any chaos that can be conjured up, would proceed to elicit significance by abstraction, analysis and organization, to introduce order by conceptual classification and categorical deletion of the real, and would, through learning from accumulated experience, anticipate the future in ways which increasingly satisfy its practical intent.[8]

One might quarrel with the phrase, "any chaos that can be conjured up" by saying that the conjurable cannot be chaotic, except in some comparative sense, but that would just reinforce the point being made. Perhaps to say that mind can order any experience is the same as saying "to be is to be orderable" and I might add that I have trouble telling the difference between "being ordered" and "being orderable." The second is a statement of potential, but it is hard to conceive of that potential orderability apart from, or not arising out of, some actual structure even though perhaps unknown. It might be objected that the fact that it is hard to conceive of the world as orderable apart from its actually being ordered somehow (a variant of Aristotle's view that act is prior to potency) does not necessarily indicate anything about reality, but reflects only the limitations of the conceivable. And at the very least, that much would have to be granted — that the three laws of thought represent a general limitation on our capacity to make intelligible. Whether they also represent a more general limitation on the real itself is the important question. I am inclined to a realism of some sort because conceivability and intelligibility appear at bottom to be affairs of structure and order and the laws of thought would appear to apply not only to conceptual structure but to structure in general. But it may be asked, how else could it be for a creature for whom conceivability and intelligibility are criteria of the real? And with that I am back in a solipsistic rationality which creates its interpretive models out of whole cloth. And from a point of view which takes the theoretical as primary and the base from which practice is carried out, this conclusion may seem final. But if practice is considered the basic context, where inside and outside, conception and world, come together, such a conclusion is wholly unacceptable simply because it renders practice itself, and especially the scientific practice of prediction and control, unintelligible. Within the context of purposive activity the conceptual and the structural are to be seen as aspects of the one reality of practice and not to be reduced to the two poles as separate parts. To do so is to deal with abstractions with no way of passing from one to the other. Within the context of purposive activity, however, the interrelation of these aspects is continuous and structured or else practice is impossible.

We shall consider the implications of the primacy of practice further later on, but the foregoing considerations do emphasize objective structure as an enabling condition, a presupposition of purposive activity or practice. Notice again, this does not constitute a theoretical proof that the world is structured or that the laws of thought apply to structure in general and not only to conceptual structure. Structure is a presupposition of practice, and the laws of thought are presuppositions of practice, but whether the latter apply to structure is unclear. It would seem to be so, however, since the structure of the world against which I practice has to be intelligible to me to permit such practice. Again, practice requires that I think of it in that way, and that is a practical proof.

Now let us gather all this together and see what has been said. Activity or practice is purposive, fallible, experimental, critical, reasoned, corrigible, meaningful, educable, and judgmental, and it involves response to a challenge, requires the distinction between real and ideal and has certain enabling conditions (presuppositions) one of which is freedom of choice. There are five other of these enabling conditions. Because activity or practice is centered around a self or agent who initiates and controls it and because it reaches out to an end or goal to complete it, these enabling conditions fall into two groups of three; *choice, concern,* and *consistency* around the controlling self and *multiplicity, continuity,* and *structure* around the end or goal aimed at. Unless these enabling conditions are present, activity or practice, having the characteristics just listed, cannot possibly come about.

The importance of these enabling conditions cannot be overemphasized. No one can exercise the three inner conditions for anyone else. But all of our practice either restricts or enlarges the alternatives for further practice for others as well as ourselves. A jail sentence does not take away my freedom of choice, it limits the available alternatives for its exercise. Brainwashing techniques developed within the last generation appear to breakdown and even rearrange the three inner conditions of the self by radically restructuring the outer conditions of the prisoner's world. It is one thing when external conditions remove the possibility of practice, it is quite another when you, in your practice, undercut those possibilities for yourself as well as for others. Just as the laws of thought are normative for that special kind of purposive practice called thinking, so there are similar conditions which are normative, obligatory for all practice no matter what the goal may be. It is the maintenance of these enabling conditions of practice that is constitutive of responsible personhood. It is this capacity in each of us to practice and by reflecting upon such practice to recognize the enabling conditions of it as obligatory that constitutes the moral dimension of human nature.

In the chapters to come we want to argue that moral responsibility is grounded in the obligation to maintain the enabling conditions of purposive activity. Freedom of choice makes their maintenance as well as their destruction possible. In the next chapter we will consider the dimensions of practice. First, the acquisitive dimension that is the foundation for traditional consequential ethical theories such as self-interest and utility and wherein the concern is with the operational conditions of practice. Second, the maintenance dimension wherein deontic (duty) ethical theories, most notably that of Immanuel Kant, find location and the concern is with the pre-operational conditions of practice. It is important to make clear the difference between these two dimensions and their respective operational and pre-operational conditions. In my experience, most so-called practical people focus primarily on the operational, how-to, aspects of their practice either assuming or ignoring the pre-operational conditions of practice itself. Perhaps this is due in part because we want to know what we have done wrong so we can block out that possibility for future action and frame a better operating procedure. But that alone is never sufficient and never gets down to the morality of practice because quite often a certain way of operating is wrong not because of its consequences but because it destroys the conditions of operating at all. All of the conditions of practice are not expressible in operational rules precisely because some of those conditions make the operational aspect of practice possible. Taken together these two sets of conditions, the operational and the pre-operational, can be considered as the necessary and sufficient conditions of practice.

Footnotes

1. New York: The Macmillan Company, 1965.

2. Ibid., p. 21.

3. Ibid., pp. 21-25.

4. Ibid., p. 26f.

5. *Values and Imperatives*, Lewis, Clarence I., John Lange, Ed., Stanford, CA: Stanford University Press, 1969, p. 124.

6. Castell, pp. 37, 48ff.

7. Classroom remark, 1948.

8. Charles Scribner's Sons, New York: 1929, p. 391

The Dimensions of Practice

CHAPTER 3

The Acquisitive Dimension

In the previous chapter the chief characteristics of business practice were set forth and also the presuppositions without which practice would not be possible. It was also pointed out that practice is bi-polar, that is, it centers around a control function and reaches toward the acquisition of some end. We will refer to this end-directedness of practice as the Acquisitive Dimension even though the ends of practice are often understood in ways other than "acquiring." Actually, this dimension is spoken about in differing ways according to what aspect of end-directed practice we wish to emphasize: in business, "buying" something or "selling" it falls easily under the acquisitive, but when we "join" an existing project we don't "acquire," we become one with. When we travel to Chicago we don't "acquire," we reach, Chicago. Also "developing" a product differs from "acquiring" one. So by the Acquisitive Dimension we will mean that some state, capacity or thing not now present to or part of the practicing self is aimed at without specifying the exact way it will be made present. Just what ends are "good" and how to determine their "goodness" as well as how to relate means to ends are primary concerns of the acquisitive dimension of practice as well as of traditional ethical theory. This purposiveness or reach of practice presupposes some goal, not any one in particular, but some goal and it is only in the purposive context of the Acquisitive Dimension, only when some end is being pursued, that any moral considerations arise at all.

Suppose you have decided upon the end to be acquired, say, going to the public library, then there are several things to be done, depending upon where you are, to get there. These several things are related to arriving at the library as means are related to ends. Any failure in choosing and implementing the necessary means signals failure with the end aimed at. It is in choosing and implementing means to ends aimed at that the control pole of practice comes into play. This means-ends way of thinking is very much in use by most of us at all times. It forms the backbone of one of the most important ethical theories in our tradition. This view is called Utilitarianism and it holds that the morality of an act is a function of its consequences. For a Utilitarian an act is "right" if its consequences are "good" and "wrong" if they are not. If you ask, as you must, what is this good that my right acts ought to lead to, the Utilitarian replies that what is good is happiness. What we ought to do is produce "the greatest amount of happiness for the greatest number of people." This is the principle upon which, during the last century in England and the United States, most of the social reform and welfare legislation has rested. Utilitarianism is a species of consequential moral thinking and there are others, for example, self-interest, pleasing God or profit maximization, and this concern for consequences, no matter how you conceive of their value, is the mark of the Acquisitive Dimension. The cost-benefit analysis so common to business practice, of course, falls under this consequential moral point of view. And it cannot help but be very clear from human experience in general and business practice in particular that, as a piece of moral machinery for use in decision making, this consequentialism is very powerful indeed. In matters of political and social reform, Utilitarian consequentialism is almost a complete success because very often the aim of reform is only the removal of the causes of suffering. But it does have its problems.

The first problem with consequentialism as moral theory is that it does not afford any means for determining what consequences are to be taken as valuable. Once some consequence is accepted as good or desirable then I ought to promote it, but consequentialism can not tell me why I ought to be concerned about any goal, my own self-interest, my company's profit or pleasing God. I think most of the time consequential theories assume that humans desire happiness, or to please God or whatever and then the acquisitive dimension takes on powerful meaning as the instrument for its promotion. And, I may in fact desire the value which their view promotes, but it does not follow from this that I "ought" to desire it. I believe, that moral thinking began in this consequential way but over the years with the development of our notions about the ultimate value of the individual we have had to change our moral thinking or undercut the individualism we wish to maintain. This instrumental view of moral thinking has been fostered and even epitomized in our era by the development of the scientific enterprise. Scientists themselves every so often, and quite rightly, lament the ends to which their discovered knowledge is put. This purely instrumental view of scientific method is reflected, I believe, in calling business studies "management science"; useful techniques for managing any business. Authors J. Clemens and D. Mayer of Hardwick College in their article, "Before Pickins, There Was Machiavelli," point out the utility of Machiavelli's naturalism in *The Prince* as a manual for managers on corporate takeovers:

> History has not been kind to Machiavelli. He is remembered primarily as the epitome of all things evil. But Machiavelli did not set out to legitimize wickedness. He simply described, in graphic and frequently brutal detail, how 16th century rulers managed, manipulated and led. "The Prince" is history's first "how to" manual for managers. Much of it offers cogent advice on acquisitions

and mergers—as timely today as it was more than 400 years ago.[1]

There are, of course, other interpretations of science to be had but, as the authors point out, the concern for power at the expense of all other values to which the scientific method can be put is traceable directly to Machiavelli's writings, has had a very checkered career in the social sciences because of the narrowness of its assumptions about human nature, the scientific and the social, and is still very much with us as attitude and method today.

To repeat, no foundation for duty, obligation or the moral "ought," can be found in the acquisitive dimension of practice. To discover the root of the notion of duty or obligation which is central to morality and a principle part of the meaning of responsibility, we must move to the second dimension of practice.

But it must be remembered that practice is purposive, directed toward an end, and no matter what that end may be, my own pleasure, my children's happiness, the profitability of the company for whom I manage or the well-being of the community in which I live, the framework will be the relating of means to ends and the concern for consequences. These are the legitimate and continuing concerns of the acquisitive dimension of purposive activity. Also, just because no foundation for the moral "ought" is discoverable in the consequentialism of the acquisitive dimension of practice does not remove it from an essential role in the moral. As we shall see, the moral imperative, although not grounded in the acquisitive, extends to consequential matters and plays a part in the meaning and intent of justice.

The Maintenance Dimension

That there is more to practice than just the instrumental function of the acquisitive dimension can be illustrated in common usage. Quite often people consider setting ends for themselves the means to which involve illegal, dishonest or demeaning practices. Upon discovering this and giving up such ends they refer to maintaining their good name or their integrity. And when they do this they are maintaining that there is more to engaging in a particular practice than just the desirable consequence they were attracted to before becoming fully aware of what it involved. In moral terms this is saying that the "rightness" or "wrongness" of an action is determined by something other than its results. It might well be asked "Why isn't losing ones good name or integrity just another consequence of pursuing that particular end, one that is of greater value to you than the particular end in question?" And so you reject the practice aiming at that end because you do not like its consequences. Why isn't this consequential way of handling the matter sufficient? All it requires is that you have a rank ordering of possible consequences to guide you in your choice of ends. And as long as the ends so ordered are ends external to practicing and consistent with practicing there is no problem. It is just when the choice of means or ends which conflict with practice is made that the moral concern with a dimension of practice other than the consequentialism of the Acquisitive comes into play. Losing ones good name or ones integrity is saying that ones capacity for responsible practice has been damaged in some way, that in my aiming for that particular end the necessary means undercut what we have called previously the enabling conditions of practice itself.

The most important and influential moral theory holding that morality is not a matter of consequences was developed by the German philosopher, Immanuel Kant (1724-1804). It will become clear that the position developed here is in large part Kantian. My concern, however, is putting it to use in the context of the problems under consideration rather than defending the interpretation and emphasis advanced in so doing. As will become clear, there are important differences from Kant also, but I do not want to emphasize them either since many of them stem from Kantian suggestion. However, our understanding of the nature and function of the maintenance dimension in the ethic of practice being set forth here will be best advanced by considering several specifically Kantian moral conceptions.

Kant held that moral concern is not with the happiness or unhappiness caused by an action, not with any of its consequences in fact, but with the nature of the activity itself. The central conception for him is the *good will*—one which acts not out of kindly feeling or because something is desired, but out of duty because it is your duty, out of "respect for the moral law." He begins the *Foundations of The Metaphysics of Morals*, which is about eighty pages long, and, next to Aristotle's *Nicomachean Ethics*, perhaps the most influential book on moral conduct in the western tradition, by saying:

> Nothing in the world—indeed nothing even beyond the world—can possibly be conceived which could be called good without qualification except a good will.[2]

Only the good will has intrinsic worth, is good-in-itself, even if it is unable to achieve its purposes. Happiness has value but only conditional value—if one has a good will then happiness is deserved and is good, otherwise not. All pleasures and desires as such are ethically neutral.

Even if we have reservations about this thing called "will" on the grounds that "wills don't will, people will," it is clear that Kant is referring to man's capacity to will, to initiate action, in the quote above. It is this capacity for "good willing" that leads Kant to place the ground of all value in the individual and it is this emphasis upon the individual that places Kant among the founding fathers of modern classical liberalism.

Now, with the ideas in mind that a good will is the basic moral value and that willing is good if the motive or principle of its action is respect for the moral law, we must consider one or two distinctions which Kant makes in order for us to understand this moral law in its proper context. Let us approach these distinctions by considering the question "How can willing be brought about?"

My willing may be determined by forces external to myself. For example, if I am put in prison my liberty to come and go as I wish is restricted or I may be forced to do someone's bidding through the pain of a twisted arm and the promise of more of the same if I do not do so. Also my willing can be determined by my love for my wife—one can be a prisoner of one's affections as completely as one can be addicted to drugs. Certainly one can be a slave of ones desires and passions to the distinct detriment of ones own well-being. All of these are examples of my willing or of my behavior being determined by forces external to my will. Some of them, however, are forces inside myself and some are forces outside myself. The state or condition of having the will determined by forces outside of itself Kant calls "heteronomy." The means-ends concern for consequences of the acquisitive dimension is heteronomous behavior whether of internal or external variety. And it is important because we need things, we are not self-sufficient creatures, but it is only a matter of prudence and not of morality, for Kant.

How else can the will be determined? It should be pointed out here that the classical determinist who denies human freedom of will answers this question by saying there are no other ways. The will is always heteronomously determined (Kant would say "predetermined" because my being in prison, or feeling the pain of arm-twisting or being in love or addicted or thirsty are all antecedent conditions of which the action of the will is a consequence). The good will for Kant is not only not pushed into action by pre-existing conditions,—a view which not only denies the freedom of the will but the ability of the will to initiate action—it is the direct source of our agency and can be determined by itself. The good will is autonomous and free when it is determined by the principles and conditions of its own nature. As may be expected at this point, there is a strong analogy between the principles and conditions of the Kantian will and the presuppositions and enabling conditions of purposive activity set forth previously.[3] On the Kantian view, the will is good, is autonomous, when the principle of its actions, derived by reflection, is expressive of its own nature. Such action maintains the will or the person as an autonomous source of action, as responsible, and such action is the only kind that is moral. We can now see that the duty Kant speaks of is the duty we have to ourselves as capable of autonomous willing. As we shall have occasion to see, to examine closely, and, as you may suspect from what has been said so far, such a "duty to ourselves" is not just a concern for self-development, self-preservation or self-satisfaction but for the conditions of being a self. Before doing so, however, let us return to the important distinctions Kant makes.

Central to Kant's notion of dutiful action, and parallel to the heteronomy-autonomy distinction, is that between hypothetical and categorical imperatives.[4] An imperative is a command, a directive to do or refrain from doing something or other. An hypothetical imperative tells us something is to be done because it will tend to produce a certain result. Thus, the command is conditional upon our wanting that result. Example: If you want to be healthy, then you ought to eat properly. And you can get out from under the "ought" simply by denying that you want that result. This is Kant's way of understanding the means-ends concern of the Acquisitive dimension discussed previously as well as his way of characterizing the activity of the heteronomous will. Such concern for consequences is a matter of prudence for Kant but has nothing directly to do with morality, for morality is a matter of categorical imperatives, commands which are unconditioned. Example: You ought not to lie? If you ask why shouldn't I lie, Kant would answer: out of respect for the moral law, because it is wrong. And Kant distinguishes between action outwardly in conformity with the moral law but really motivated by self-interest and action done from a sense of duty. But, if all and only moral acts are done from a sense of duty, many of us would say Kant has conceived morality too narrowly. We recognize moral acts done from love without the motive of duty being involved. However, the dual nature of consciousness mentioned before makes motivation a complex rather than a simple matter and it is generally agreed that Kant only requires that the sense of duty be present along with other motives. But he would hold that desire by itself is not a moral motive. The important point for us here is that the moral law is categorical, unconditioned and has no relation to consequences.

But Kant had another reason for not appealing to consequences which can be understood in terms of the distinction between empirical knowledge based upon observation and *a priori* knowledge. Observation can tell us what is, but not what ought to be and the moral law has a necessity which empirical knowledge cannot give us.[5] For example, we can know *a priori* that lying is wrong. How to establish this? It is wrong to tell lies because if it were right for everyone to lie, lying would become meaningless. An act is right if it can be universalized without self-contradiction. When we act on a principle which we cannot wish could become a universal law, the act is wrong. If everyone could lie there would be no truth and lying would be impossible. It is this arbitrary making of exceptions in ones own interest that is essentially immoral. Any moral decision claims universality - that is the common sense meaning of "right" - no action would be right for me unless it would be right for everyone.

On the face of it, the appeal to duty and the categorical doesn't explain anything. We feel constrained to ask "Why ought I do my duty?" and "How do I know what my duty is?" If you aren't going to appeal to consequences, how else can you explain why acts are right or wrong? To follow this line of thought we should ask ourselves "How is action related to the will or self that performs it?"

This question can best be answered, perhaps, by employing a distinction first made by Aristotle; the distinction between the actualization of a potential and the exercise of a capacity. But first we must set up this distinction in terms of the context of practice.

Within the context of purposive activity the act of choosing has direct reference to both poles of practice but the way the act of choice is related to the two poles is very different and this difference is of first importance to us. To recall, the two poles of practice are the end aimed at—the cake I am baking, the knowledge of the solar system astronomizing will yield,—and the "self", initiating, directing and controlling the activity. The act of choosing is related to the end aimed at as means are related to ends. The chief characteristic of this relation is that attaining the end is the result or the consequence of employing the means—the baking produces the cake. By virtue of the phenomenon of self-reference, the ability of the "self" to have itself as its object, the act of choosing may have this same means-end relation with itself. But it should be noted that the end is a state or condition of the "self" resulting from or brought about by employing the means—I become a pianist by practicing. Of course, this phenomenon of self-reference makes self-interest as a purposive activity possible.

But the act of choosing has another relation to the "self"-pole of a different sort. By practicing I *become* a pianist, but when I tell a lie I *am* a liar; I do not become a liar, I am one *in the telling*. I exercise my capacity to lie in the same way I exercise my capacity to speak English or to sing. These two relationships of the self to itself in the act of choice are an excellent example of the distinction between the actualization of a potential and the exercise of a capacity. By practicing I actualize my potential and become a pianist. In telling a lie I exercise a capacity I possess and am a liar. Much of modern and contemporary ethical theory centers on either one or the other of these two. If the former, then the ethics propounded are utilitarian and naturalistic. If the latter, then deontological and non-naturalistic. And in truth these school distinctions are overly simple for the line between the exercise of a capacity and the actualization of a potential is not easily drawn in any exclusive fashion. I do not practice without exercising some limited capacity already possessed as a basis for the further actualizing or upgrading of that capacity. Obviously, the difference between little Johnny whose "playing" only a doting mother could appreciate and the playing of a concert pianist is "playing well," a matter of norms and excellences in the playing of the piano.

The strong strain of naturalism in American thought under the influence of science has kept moral theory tied to a very narrow base and posed a problem for the deontologists in finding a legitimate grounding for their non-naturalistic moral duty (you can't derive the "ought" from the "is"). But if you are to understand human behavior in a theory that will be consistent with its own possibility, a naturalism broad enough to include the distinction between the potential and the actual must be made credible in spite of common sense positivism in our view of science and the real. Only in such terms can moral theory be of any use and avoid being relegated to the religious, the social, the subjective, the emotive or the linguistic. Of course, this truncated naturalism is not confined to economics, business or philosophy. Rather, it is a pervading cast to a very large part of our intellectual endeavors. Recently, with the coming of phenomenology and existentialism to our shores, there have been signs of broadening our perspective. But too often such signs turn out to be sidestepping. The more recent development of Chaos theory seems to indicate such a broadening of our naturalism and because it has arisen within the fields of science it will be harder to sidestep.

But though both of these relationships of the self to itself may be involved in carrying on purposive activity and practicing in the general sense, the importance of the distinction for an adequate understanding of activity can not be over-emphasized. Let us consider it in a classical context to bring out its importance.

In Book II of Plato's *Republic*[6], Glaucon asks Socrates to show that justice, in and of itself, is better than injustice and not merely because of its consequences. Socrates accepts the challenge but it is not clear, whatever the remainder of the *Republic* may accomplish, that he succeeds in fulfilling Glaucon's request. As we said, Kant also held that morality is not a matter of consequences, that virtuous action is not virtuous because of its consequences and he gives what may well be the most adequate reply to Glaucon's question in the whole tradition when he argues that virtuous action is virtuous when it affirms the conditions of its own possibility. It becomes vicious when it cuts the ground from under that possibility. Human beings have the capacity to carry on purposive activity in the sense in which we have been discussing it; Kant calls it "practical reason." This capacity has necessary presuppositions without which it would be impossible. One of these is freedom of choice which gives man the possibility of destroying the very conditions of that capacity. In the light of this, the Stoic dictum, "Virtue is its own reward," takes on a richer meaning and can be understood to mean that virtue maintains or continues the conditions of its own possibility. Only when these conditions are maintained can you be responsible for what you do, can you be a responsible person. Virtue, or Justice, in reference to Glaucon's request, is good-in-itself, divorced from all consequences, in that action in accord with it affirms, and in so doing maintains, the conditions of individual responsibility as a person. We shall consider this notion of Justice in a later chapter.

In these terms, morality, for Kant, is not a matter of the actualization of the potential or of the acquisitive dimension as we have called it. The moral for Kant is a function of the capacity for willing to itself. Man has desires and needs and he engages in action which hopefully will result in fulfilling these desires and needs. In fulfilling these desires and needs and actualizing his potential, he exercises his capacity to will, to choose, to engage in purposive activity. It is to Kant's credit that he saw that the actualization of a potential and the exercise of a capacity are so intimately linked that it is possible, in willing the actualization of some potential, to destroy the capacity for such willing (exercise). Put somewhat differently, because willing involves choice, the exercise of the capacity to will can, to use a contemporary phrase, "self-destruct," one can vote away ones right to vote.

Morality becomes a matter of the maintenance of the enabling conditions of the exercise of the capacity of willing which we have called "purposive activity." This means that along with whatever external ends any activity may have in view and along with whatever hypothetical imperatives such ends may require, there is a set of enabling conditions of activity which can be destroyed through choice or lack of it and must be preserved. They are the basic norms of practice and we shall consider their status presently. But the point now is that underlying the acquisitive dimension of practice is the maintenance of the enabling conditions of such practice. And the criterion for determining whether any proposed action undercuts these conditions is whether a proposed action is consistent with the conditions of its own possibility; that is, a proposed action would be right if it could be a principle upon which all rational beings as members of an intelligible world, including myself, could practice without destroying that capacity. Lying would be a right *choice* only if I could be a *concerned* and *consistent* liar. Such a requirement would completely destroy the conditions for the exercise of the capacity of willing, of engaging in purposive activity. The individual's first duty is to practice in accordance with the principles of his own being as capable of willing, as a person who is responsible for his own activity. Action on any other grounds, either determination by external ends or by inner desires reduces practice to process, freedom to some form of outer slavery or inner bondage and completely undercuts responsibility. Certainly, it is the case that such freedom of choice is a matter of degree and is not absolute in its usage, but the capacity is there or I couldn't do what I am doing.

It is one thing when external conditions remove the possibility of purposive activity, it is quite another when you in your own actions undercut those possibilities for yourself as well as for others. Just as the laws of thought are normative for that special kind of purposive activity called thinking, so there are similar conditions which are normative and obligatory for practice as well. It is the maintenance of these conditions of practice which is constitutive of responsible personhood. It is this capacity in each of us to carry on purposive activity and by reflecting upon such activity, to recognize the enabling conditions of it as obligatory, that constitutes the moral dimension of human nature. As we said earlier, Kant calls this capacity "practical reason" and characterizes its enabling condition as "categorical" and unconditionally imperative. This doesn't mean that you are compelled to do something, you have the power of choice and can do otherwise, but it does mean that you *ought* to do something on pain of undercutting your own nature as a responsible person if you do not and the "ought" is unconditional.

The considerations just mentioned lead to one of the most important and striking aspects of this view of the responsibility of natural persons. Simply put, the enabling conditions which maintain the possibility for me to be responsible are the conditions which maintain the possibility for all persons to be responsible. For example, as previously noted, freedom of choice itself requires the presence of real alternatives for choice and maintaining such alternatives for ourselves maintains them for others also.

A good example of this idea comes from an understanding of the old slogan "Support Your Better Business Bureau" and the realization of how this can best be done. It is widely recognized that the best way to give such support is to conduct your business affairs in an honest manner because by so doing you establish a climate in which other businesses and your own can do likewise. In short, the conditions which best support you in your corporate practice are the ones which best support all corporate practice. We are all involved in maintaining the conditions of personal responsibility for ourselves as well as for others. It would seem that this is the primary and supportive relationship of society to its members and of the members to each other and to themselves. Off hand, I can think of no duties founded on other grounds than these.

Let me give further example of how these enabling conditions function reciprocally in various communal relations closer to home. If, in conducting my class, my views are stated dogmatically and with finality, I am open to being made a fool of if anyone shows that my views need modification and this in turn casts doubts upon my knowledge of the materials in question as well as whether I am adequately concerned with and reasonably consistent in what I am about. Is my choice of opinions generally in keeping with the relevant facts? Does it reflect sensible concern for other opinion in the area? If not, it could be argued that I am not acting as a responsible person in my teaching. But at the same time consider the situation in which my students find themselves. In the face of such dogmatism, they have two alternatives. Either they agree with me and learn nothing, or they disagree with me and are dead as far as success in the class is concerned. Either way they lose. The conditions which enable my being reasonable enable everyone else in the class to be reasonable. Even closer to home, consider the conditions of responsible personhood in the family situation. If the parents maintain those enabling conditions in their family life, then the children, or anyone living there, can benefit from their exercise in their own activities. If it be objected that this is because in both examples someone is in authority and sets the tone, it can be pointed out that the same situation pertains between any two people carrying on a conversation. Most conversations break down because one or the other or both persons fail to maintain the conditions which enable the conversational activity to continue. A principal part of the value of friendship and the family resides in supplying just such a supportive context. Towards the end of the last century in the United States, the railroads had to request outside regulation because the "cut-throat" competition in which they were engaged was destroying the enabling conditions of competition itself; enter the Interstate Commerce Commission as external regulator.

In an article in the *Harvard Business Review* entitled, "Can the Executive Afford a Conscience," Albert L. Carr, in discussing what steps an executive could take to make his own moral principles palatable to his organization writes as follows:

> In essence, any ethically oriented proposal made to a manager is a proposal to take a longer-range view of his problem... The longer range a realistic business projection is, the more likely it is to find sound ethical footing. I would go so far as to say that almost anything an executive does, on whatever level, to extend the range of thinking of his superiors tends to effect an ethical advance... The hope and the opportunity of the individual executive with a contemporary conscience lies in the constructive connection of the long-run economic view with the socially aware outlook.[7]

I do not know what theoretical justification Mr. Carr would give for his judgment that as self-interest is pursued on a long-run basis it tends to become congruent, or at least asymptotic, with the morally acceptable, but the differences between the enabling conditions and the consequences of practice, noted previously, and the fact that as soon as your aim is beyond the short-run of direct consequences, it takes on concern for the enabling conditions of future consequences, would appear to be adequate for the task. In the short-run, a manager can do a good deal about direct consequences but little if anything about the enabling conditions that are already in place in the present. In the long-run, the situation is reversed and a great deal can be done about the enabling conditions of future consequences.

And, as pointed out before, concern for enabling conditions is not limited to concern for my interests only, because they are the conditions of all self-interest including my own.

The points I wish to make here are (1) that these enabling conditions are common to the interests of everyone, and (2) that no matter what our self-interest may be, we have a vested interest in these enabling conditions being in place simply because without them self-interested activity could not come about. The phrase "self-interest" is ambiguous in its meaning. Sometimes it refers to whatever a self may be interested in, my friend's well-being, the profitability of the company I work for or my own health. Sometimes it is meant more narrowly to mean that at bottom people are only interested in themselves. On this narrow view, the interests of people are naturally mutually exclusive and there are no grounds for concern with others, no foundation at all for morality. There is a considerable amount of classical and neo-classical economic opinion to the effect that self-interest can operate in a vacuum without benefit of supporting conditions. From the perspective taken here, self-interest, in either of the two senses, is not an atomic phenomenon but requires that the enabling conditions be in place.

It is just here that Professor Friedman's view seems to be inadequate. In his article, "The Social Responsibility of Business Is to Increase Its Profits,"[8] he wants to maintain that the self-interest of the owners is the proper concern of the corporate executive and that what may be thought to be socially beneficial is never his concern. The manager has no "social responsibilities." But while there are many interests that a self-interested person may have, there are also some interests that a self-interested person "ought" to have; the conditions enabling self-interest, his own or anyone else's. And these conditions are both social and individual in a sense which Friedman's viewpoint would not seem to allow. Surely, it is in the "public" interest in a capitalistic society to enact laws to maintain the enabling conditions of self-interested practice. That is what freedom is all about. And in the absence of such laws the individual citizen, executive or otherwise, is morally obligated to maintain those conditions no matter what other ends may be served as well. There is nothing socialistic about that nor is it a matter of the aggregate of the self-interests in the community at any specific time (majority rule). Communities as well as individuals can be wrong about these matters at the peril of their own self-interests.

The distinction we have made between purposive practice and the need to maintain the enabling conditions of such practice suggests some comments upon the Invisible Hand of Adam Smith which seem appropriate in this context. Smith held, you will remember, that if each individual pursues his own self-interest under equal market conditions, each individual will be

> led by an invisible hand to promote an end which was no part of his intention. Nor is it always the worse for the society that it was no part of it. By pursuing his own interests, he frequently promotes that of his society more effectively than when

> he really intends to promote it. I have never known much good done by those who affected to trade for the public good.[9]

One cannot help wondering what considerations recommended this view to Smith. That what is in my interest should be in the interest of the community might be true by chance sometimes, but he obviously isn't speaking of chance occurrences. As a general rule, however, it is obviously false. Some light can be shed, I believe, in terms of the distinction made between self-interest and the enabling conditions of self-interest. Adequate self-interest requires concern for the presuppositions of self-interested practice. In the above passage, Smith may be understood as saying that concern for the enabling conditions of self-interested practice is most adequate in the context of self-interested practice. And because those conditions are common to all, the well-being of the entire community is promoted unintentionally. Surely, in these terms, Smith's "invisible hand" remarks merit more serious consideration than they are usually accorded.

Nor is Smith alone in thinking along these lines. James Madison, in considering the problem of "factions" in our democratic society in *The Federalist* (paper #10), conceives of our representative form of government as having something like the beneficial effect of the Invisible Hand. As long as the factions in the society remain small in size and large in number, they tend to cancel each other out, allowing a kind of balance and equilibrium through competition to be maintained beneficial to the whole. As with the economic model of activity, the conditions that threaten this classic position are the conditions that tend to introduce inequalities into the political and economic contexts; unfair advantages, control of markets and constituencies, and inequalities of size and staying power. No doubt the conditions of the Industrial Revolution worked exactly in that fashion to keep Smith's classic situation off balance. Even if the Industrial Revolution had not supplied these inequalities, a case can be made that the conditions for Smith's Invisible Hand are ideal and subject to many qualifications in practice some of which are no doubt shown in the history of our political and economic institutions.

But there is more to this than the savagery of competition in the economic and the mechanical canceling of votes in the political to keep the balance. Kant held that his first formulation of the categorical imperative, "act only according to that maxim by which you can at the same time will that it should become a universal law,"[10] which says nothing about the good of others, was completely consistent with his third formulation, "act so as to treat humanity both in your own person and that of every other always as an end and never as a means only,"[11] which explicitly concerns the good of others. All three of these men, Smith most explicitly perhaps, are expressing their insight that, self-interest if rationally pursued, would involve the preservation of its own enabling conditions. To say that all three are 18th Century rationalists is to say at least that they took these enabling conditions for granted or as self-evident in the same way Locke and Jefferson took human rights. The fact that we have discovered that these enabling conditions are neither self-evident nor should they ever be taken for granted does not vitiate Smith's insight that the well-being of the community of self-interested persons and the self-interest of individual practice are one and the same, identical, in the matter of these enabling conditions. Another way of saying this is that while all three of these men grew up in the climate of Enlightenment individualism, the rationalism which all three espouse pushes them, Kant explicitly, Smith in his Invisible Hand view and Madison also, to include the social as an essential ingredient in individualism and not in conflict with it. In a less public source, Madison says further:

> Is there no virtue among us? If there be not, no form of government will render us secure. To suppose that any form of government will secure liberty or happiness without virtue in the people is a chimerical idea.[12]

What he means by virtue is "the permanent and aggregate interests of the community."[13] I take it that "aggregate interests" refers to interests arising in each and every person and, therefore, common to the community. These include, I believe, what I have been calling the enabling conditions of practice.

Historical speculation aside, however, the well-being of a community of persons free to practice in their own self-interest requires the maintenance of these enabling conditions. And a principle part of the practice of persons, managers and corporations ought to be devoted to their strengthening on pain of having the foundations of our practice "molder in dust away."

Current criticism of managerial practice charges that American business is short-sighted in its practice, i.e., the automotive industry in its recent failure in the competitive market. The reasons given why this is so run from the connection between needed financial support and stock market quotations to the short terms of office of top executives. While such external conditions may contribute, one of the reasons for this short-sightedness may well be in the way people in business are brought up to think about these matters, the structure of the market system in classical economics. In the market system, the degree to which the ideal of pure competition is attained is the degree to which an equilibrium of the forces of self-interest can be maintained. The question becomes who or what aims at preserving the conditions of pure competition? And there is much ambiguity in the answers given. Most often it is assumed that each individual in the market system is pursuing his own self- interest, in the narrow sense, and this means only government is available to preserve the conditions of pure competition. Our own history shows that this leads, slowly but surely, to increased control by government and the slow change from a market to a command economy.

Our political system rests upon the idea of a community of self-governing persons. This must include, as part of its rationality, the preservation of its own enabling conditions. The theory of our economic system, however, makes no such assumption about self-government, or if it does, self-government is equated with fulfilling wants, of maximizing what is of profit to the individual. This view makes use of reason only in the instrumental sense and makes no provisions for the conditions of its own maintenance. This view condemns all economic thought to the short-run, is counter to the political theory of self- government, and in its operation slowly undercuts its own possibility for reasons we have seen.

Looking ahead, we have seen that practice is critical, performed with reference to criteria, and this means that activity is value dependent, that is, there are norms that are imperative for practice. Differing activities are regulated by and even constituted by the norms peculiar to them. The rules of chess are constitutive of the game, as are the rules of baseball. The distinction being made parallels the established distinction between the descriptive and prescriptive functions of concepts. The definition of "pencil" as a thin cylinder of wood, six to eight inches long, surrounding a lead-graphite center used for writing, not only describes the features of a pencil, but also prescribes those features anything must have if it is to be a pencil. This latter is the prescriptive function of the concept "pencil." The difference between a pencil and a person is that a person is capable of recognizing and conceiving of this prescriptive aspect of his own nature and functioning. As such, this prescriptive function becomes normative for the person and the degree to which the norms are supported in practice is the degree to which the integrity, the capacities as a person, are maintained. And to support these norms for ones own practice is to support them for everyone else. The degree to which a person's practice undercuts these norms is the degree to which the integrity, this capacity to practice, to be free and responsible in his functioning as a person, is being destroyed. Of course, the concept "pencil" has nothing necessary about it even though it is a useful one. In fact, I suspect, a pencil is just a pencil and the prescriptive and descriptive aspects, two different ways of looking at the nature of pencil, become evident only for a subject who, for the sake of practice, has to be able to describe the end aimed at as well as judge with what success the end aimed at is being realized, whether that end is writing, fishing or studying the stars. This is not to suggest for a moment that the grounds for this distinction lie in the subject and not in the pencil; knowing is an activity also, bi-polar in nature and having its presuppositions. But the point is that the context of practice is the locus both of what is and what ought to be. It is only when the context of practice in neglected that the "is-ought" gap arises.

Now, by way of summary, I have presented a conception of activity or practice that is purposive, reflective and presuppositioned. I have been concerned primarily with the latter characteristics, the presuppositions of practice, as the locus of obligation and the source of responsibility, and have called this aspect the Maintenance dimension of practice. Freedom of choice brings about concern with moral matters of maintenance. And in the light of this, purposive activity is seen to be two dimensional. No matter to what external end activity may be directed, for example, managing, there are the conditions of activity itself that must be maintained. Perhaps this requirement is best expressed in Kant's third formulation of the categorical imperative: "act so as to treat humanity, both in your own person and in that of every other, as an end and never as a means only." In the context of practice and with respect to our treatment of others and ourselves, this statement very nearly says it all. But to treat anyone as an end requires you to maintain the enabling conditions of responsible practice for that person. Nothing else will do it.

Footnotes

1. N.Y. Times Business Section, 2 Mar. '86, p. 3.

2. New York: The Liberal Arts Press, Inc.,1959, L.W.Beck, tr., p.9. Hereafter, FMM.

3. In fact, the enabling conditions of practice began as a generalization upon Kant's Presuppositions of Practical Reason; cf. *The Worlds of Hume and Kant,* H. Allen and J. Wilbur; 2nd Rev. Edition, Buffalo, NY: Prometheus Books, 1982, p. 148.

4. FMM, p.31.

5. Ibid., p.37.

6. 365-367.

7. July-August, 1970, p. 64.

8. N.Y. Times Magazine, 9/12/70, cited previously.

9. *The Wealth of Nations*, Bk. IV, Ch. ii, Cannon Edition, London, 1930, p. 421.

10. FMM, p. 39.

11. FMM, p. 47.

12. Quoted in *Habits of the Heart*, Bellah, R.N. et al, New York: Harper & Row, 1985, pp. 254-5. Hereafter HH.

13. *The Federalist*, #10, New York; Random House, The Modern Library, 1937, p. 54.

The Enabling Conditions: Applications I

CHAPTER 4

In the last chapter, the importance of the enabling conditions of the maintenance dimension for the possibility of practice was pointed out and discussed. Some examples of their function in business and in individual practice were given along with their consideration against an historical background. In this chapter I want to consider the importance of these enabling conditions of practice in the broader framework of American society and as, in part, an answer to questions raised in three current studies. The first of the three is that excellent book *Habits of the Heart* by Robert N. Bellah and company.[1]

The title of the book, *Habits of the Heart*, derives from de Tocqueville's famous *Democracy in America* and the book itself is a study of "individualism," a term first used by de Tocqueville in describing life in America. The authors of the present study mark out four varieties of individualism having a place in our history and continuing expression in our culture[2] : the biblical tradition, dominant in early New England but still very much with us, exemplified in the puritan John Winthrop; the republican tradition, exemplified by Thomas Jefferson and deriving in its modern form from Locke and the Enlightenment; Utilitarianism, exemplified by Ben Franklin and destined to become the dominant model in our time; and Expressive Individualism, exemplified by Walt Whitman and the subjective and expressive counterpart of the Utilitarian. In each of these four we find the emphasis and value upon the individual but surrounded by other elements; the individual as acceptable in God's sight, the individual as citizen, the individual as a success in this life and the individual whose preferences are fulfilled. All four of the varieties are purposive in nature, that is, they have a generalized notion of the good at which individuals aim. All four, as you might expect, employ a means-ends way of thinking as well as the instrumental use of reason in pursuing those ends. All four contain as major ends the ideals of success, freedom and justice but the meanings given to these ends vary according to the company they keep. Nevertheless, the authors' claim that strands of individualism from all four varieties are present and alive in our contemporary society. It will be obvious that the position developed in the opening chapters here is also an individualism but one which differs from the four varieties in *Habits of the Heart* not by contradicting them so much as being presupposed by them. The sense in which this is so can best be brought out by looking at the major differences between the four varieties of individualism.

The major difference lies between the first two and the last two; biblical and republican individualism both have a reference beyond the individual. In the biblical, it is John Winthrop's "city set upon a hill," a spiritual community, the authority for whose virtues lies in the word of God. In the republican, it is Thomas Jefferson's self-governing republic, the authority for whose virtues lies in reason and the common interests of mankind. In the last two, utilitarian and expressive individualism, modern individualism comes into its own, unrelated to anything but itself, first, in Franklin's rules for success of the financial sort with its authority residing in the needs and interests of the individual and second, in Whitman's "I celebrate myself" with its possibilities for experience and its authority residing in subjective feeling. These latter two are dominant and are, in a sense, the outside and inside of what the authors call the ontological individualism of modern contemporary America; the struggle for success in the external world and the search for fulfillment and wholeness in the inner life. [It is quite possible that in the short statement just given of these four varieties of individualism, justice has hardly been done. It is hoped, however, that the sins are largely of omission due to the need for summary and not of commission by dint of misstatement.]

In the previous chapters, an individualism has been set out by us not unlike the individualism of *Habits of the Heart.* The acquisitive dimension of practice is concerned with success, the maintenance dimension, with freedom. A concern for justice as the practicing relationship between these two dimensions will come along later on. From the early modern to the present there have been developments touching these varieties of individualism, actually one under-cutting the other, as the modern world comes into being; the authority of the biblical tradition is undercut by the success of reason wedded to experience through measurement in classical science and the objective certainty of classical reason in the republican tradition is undercut by the subjective and relativistic aspects of the appeal to individual experience. And at that point modern individualism, having confused being an individual with being a particular, undercuts itself in emptiness and isolation, exactly as de Tocqueville feared it would when he visited us in the 1830's.

The view of the individual presented here is of an organic activity, a "being" in the dynamic sense of that term, a view which, I believe, *Habits of the Heart* intends also. But organic activity does not come about either internally or externally *in* vacuo and that peculiarly human kind of organic activity which we have called practice requires the exercise of certain capacities and the presence of certain conditions both internally and externally. The capacities may be presumed in humans here but they need exercise and development. The conditions, both internal (the open mind) and external (the open community), are only partially present and require constant attention both inside and outside to cope with and accommodate our changing selves and world. But this organic capacity for action, this freedom, can undercut itself and destroy itself if not handled sensibly. There are built-in limits to its continuation and efficacy. As I read and studied *Habits of the Heart*, I waited in vain for the recognition of these necessary conditions and when Madison was quoted concerning the necessity of virtue in the citizens to make the republican form of government successful I was hopeful, but to no avail. The authors even go to the ecological framework as the conditions enabling life and carry it one step further by talking about "a social ecology," but the connection is never made between the conditions of such an ecology and the possibility of successful human individualism. In this work I am concerned about the possibility of full-fledged human individualism and the conditions without which it cannot come to be. Individual practice that is not aware of the need to maintain the conditions of its own possibility is undercutting itself as well as everyone else because the conditions are the same for all individual practice. I think that in slightly different language, but still, I believe, in what the authors call "the primary language," the message of *Habits of the Heart* is that American individualism has lost its sense of community and any grounds for authority beyond self-interest. We are told to consider our older biblical and republican traditions but also that the grounds for community in those traditions, respectively religious faith and reason, must be modified to suit present sensibilities. I think they are correct about the importance of those traditions for us and the need for the modification of something, and the individualism put forward here is of the self-conscious kind that recognizes the conditions of its own possibility. But let us back off for a minute and consider these matters from a little different perspective.

In *Habits of the Heart* the authors hold that the two modern varieties of individualism, utilitarian and expressive, "are incapable of sustaining either a public or a private life."[3] Their judgment is, and the rest of the book buttresses it, that "perhaps only the civic and biblical forms of individualism—forms that see the individual in relation to a larger whole, a community and a tradition—are capable of sustaining genuine individuality and nurturing both public and private life."[4]

The first thing to say about this concerns the "relation to a larger whole." Here we are talking about commitment to something other than the individual itself and from the individualistic point of view it looks as if such commitment is antithetical to and a restriction upon individual freedom and autonomy. And it is part of the human situation that commitment involves limitation; human activity always involves committing yourself to something not yet attained and in so doing limiting, even risking, what you already are. Sometimes the risk factor is large, sometimes small, but always present.

The utilitarian and expressive forms of individualism were found unsatisfactory because the former as the search for success in terms of money and keeping up with the Jones' is endless and empty, and the latter, as continuing fulfillment of individual preferences, is meaningless. These two are unsatisfactory as forms of individualism because acting on them alone or even together conveys no sense of identity or meaning upon the actor; the very center of the whole idea of personality in individualism is missing.

If the above is an adequate assessment, then we should ask: What do the biblical and civic forms of individualism have that the other two don't that confer meaning and identity upon those committed to them? The only way that the particular content of my experience at any time takes on any meaning for me is through the interpretive act of relating what is present to what is not now present but related to what is present in some specific ways. Simply put, I relate what I see to what I understand and what I understand always goes beyond what I see. A person suffering from amnesia has to build a meaningful life all over again because the sense of identity, of who you are, is lost; there is no past, no "community of memory," to borrow from *Habits of the Heart*, to give meaning and identity to the present. A good part of our sense of self is constituted by that with which we identify ourselves. The next question is: What are the biblical and civic committed to that convey identity and meaning upon those committed to them without limiting and restricting their autonomy and their individualism? Here, I can only return to the much maligned self-interest inherent in individualism and say that what they have in common is that they make evident, no matter what else they do, the conditions which enable any self-interested activity and, when followed, constitute a community of responsible persons. Both the civic and the biblical traditions contain and supply the conditions of commitment, of meaning and personal identity, which, insofar as they are recognized, accepted and sustained in practice "preserve and enlarge freedom," to borrow a phrase. In the civic tradition, these conditions founded upon human possibility are to be extended to all through human effort and the realization of an ideal world city and any look at history makes clear the manifold risks to which this endeavor is continuously subjected. In the biblical tradition, these conditions, founded also in human possibility are buttressed by God as creator and assured of fulfillment by His guidance and intent. As ultimate ideals for commitment there are many questions for both traditions. However, insofar as these traditions, one basically Greco-Roman and the other Judeo-Christian, have fostered the view of human possibility expressed in these enabling conditions, they have much to say to us about individualism. And insofar as humans in these traditions have conceived, practiced and experienced living in the light of these possibilities and found them to preserve, enlarge, and constitute much that is most desirable in our idea of individualism, then we don't need to modify the traditions, biblical and civic, so much as we need to come to a more adequate idea of individualism.

In a somewhat narrower framework because its focus is upon the political and yet broader in that it encompasses a larger historical context, Ralph Ketcham, in his recent book, *Individualism and Public Life: A Modern Dilemma*,[5] does an excellent job with the same problem. In his Preface, he refers to Leonard Silk, economics editor for The New York Times (sometime during the summer of 1985, I presume):

> Silk suggests that the United States in the 1980s might need to depend less on individuals and groups motivated by self-interest and more on "civic spirit, morality, benevolence, and a concern for the well-being of others" in its public

> life. I hope in this essay to lay out the origins and dimensions of the outlook (individualism) Silk finds so problematic, to probe for insights by looking at a culture (East Asian Confucianism) that makes different assumptions about human relationships and public life, and then to suggest altered guidelines for concepts of citizenship, for leadership and for making political decisions."[6]

I have nothing but appreciation for the breadth and depth of his analysis and history covering both Greek and Judeo-Christian sources of the problem of individualism as well as his analysis and comparison of Confucianism with it. It is good reading, instructive and to be recommended. But I want to look at his "altered guidelines" in the light of the ideas developed in this book.

Having given a fine account of how and in what form individualism arrives at the present, he writes:

> ...the American tradition, liberal, atomistic and individualistic, validates this cacophony of interests, passions and impulses as fair, democratic, and, in a way, even purposeful. Somehow the interplay of diverse forces and interests is raised to a level of principle which becomes a surrogate for the spirit of the nation. But can such an (anti?) principle really serve as the spirit, or public philosophy, of the nation?"[7]

> "The United States confronts, perhaps for the first time in its history, not a need to fine tune, enlarge, reapply or update its individualist ideology, but rather the limitations of the ideology itself."[8]

By way of contrast with our individualistic tradition Professor Ketcham refers to Aristotle who starts with human beings as social animals to begin with, but the real contrast comes in the analysis of the Confucianism undergirding East Asian societies in that human beings are understood, therein, in a relational way that makes them elements in a network of social relationships centering on the community or state. His discussion of in what sense societies founded on such assumptions can ever be democratic or even industrial in ways comparable to our own is enlightening and to the point. But it remains a serious question how such an other-directed orientation can be grafted onto our self-directed view. This is another perspective on the problem of commitment previously considered in *Habits of the Heart.* The civic model, we found there, is central to Ketcham's concern for public life and, with Jefferson, again, as the model, he analyses the republican tradition:

> In this model a person becomes a responsible citizen in so far as he or she, through education, moral instruction, occupational influence, political practice, and conscientious resolve, is able to curb selfish tendencies, and instead achieve in some degree a public perspective."[9]

The growth of the idea that political and decision processes are to consist in the activity of brokering divergent interests, that began with Martin Van Buren in the first Jackson campaign and has continued to the present, is considered and found wanting in that it contains no view of the public good and is more often than not short-sighted. Instead of this "flawed brokering"

> let us suppose, as the civic concept does, that the office of the citizen requires people to be in some degree disinterested, to have some capacity to see the common good, and to find in willing participation in public life an important fulfillment of their own lives."[10]

Without being able to do full justice to them here, the "altered guidelines" suggested in the above passage are "disinterestedness,"[11] and "concern for the public good."[12] But how bring about this altered orientation alongside of the self-interest orientation? The suggested method is by education[13] and as an example of what these altered attitudes can accomplish, Professor Ketcham cites the negotiations, lasting twenty years, that produced the Law of the Sea Treaty.

> Meeting under United Nations auspices and thus without a sovereignty to settle process or substance, the negotiating conference had to devise its own rules and was free to find its own solutions.[14]

> The result was a surprisingly open and creative search both for the accommodation of interests all knew could not be steamrollered, and for the transcendence of the particular to recognize the common good.[15]

> The law of the sea negotiations suggest, ..., that the individualist-based political axioms so customary and so celebrated in the United States are not the only ones available.[16]

The conclusion is that our individualism must become "more socially oriented" in terms of the disinterestedness and concern for the public good set forth previously and exemplified in the law of the sea treaty negotiations. But how do you teach and develop these guidelines without giving the impression that you are imposing an interest from the outside, the common good, that doesn't necessarily have any relation to my own interests or that somehow I am supposed to become "disinterested?" I suspect that concern for the sea itself, as our concern with ecology, presents a common interest and condition for all particular interests and that recognition of this was a large step in the proper direction. The idea of disinterestedness arose in the Age of Reason to characterize the results of reason in contrast to individual self-interest as motive. If the deliverances of reason are universal in scope, 2 + 2 = 4 for everyone and not anyone in particular only, then in so far as persons are rational, they are disinterested and not self-interested. This view received its most interesting application as lending objectivity to the experience of aesthetic values, particularly in Kant and Schopenhauer, but it was primarily a way of looking at reason as operating outside the framework of human desire. Should one wonder about the connection between aesthetics and reason, perhaps it will suffice in passing to note that the criteria for reasoning are all aesthetic. Since that age, our faith in reason to deliver the truth and in the objectivity of values has taken a terrible beating, but in Ketcham's usage, I believe it serves the same function; it detaches the self from interests of its own and lends objectivity to the value of the common good.

My own suggestion is that if you want to teach the attitude Professor Ketcham thinks necessary, you can do so very effectively by reflecting upon the practice of self-interest of any sort, itself, and the conditions that make it possible, both in the individual and in the social context, as I have been doing here. It is not difficult to produce the realization that the conditions that allow me to practice self-interestedly allow everyone to practice self-interestedly. The search to make those enabling conditions explicit will take me a long way into a public good that is of interest to me because it is seen to be indispensable to the possibility of interested practice by anyone, including me. That all humans have this capacity of reflective reason, that it is one of the major sources of their values and standards and that a fundamental concern of education is to exercise, strengthen and develop this capacity is central to our ideas of responsible individuality. I am not really disagreeing with Professor Ketcham's analysis or with what he would like to bring about. I am only suggesting that an adequate conception of individualism, one that will include concern for the enabling conditions of its own possibility, will go a long way toward achieving a common good that I am interested in as an integral part of my self-interest. This is not to say that a benevolence and concern for others is not possible and, even desirable, but it is to say that an adequate self-interest is the best foundation for and in no way antithetical to the public good as exemplified in these enabling conditions. And while in this context, it is appropriate to add that, while moral judgment cannot be taught in the way mathematics can be, there is a great deal that can be said about these enabling conditions as the ground of responsible practice at every level of education and it doesn't need to have anything to do with the separation between church and state. We are only talking about the foundations for our way of life and their authority lies in the use of our reflective reason and its application to the varying and changing conditions of our experience.

A further application is to be found in the book *Ethics and Profits: The Crisis of Confidence in American Business*, referred to previously, reflecting upon the problem confronting business through the lack of trust on the part of the public and suggesting how business can regain that trust. The problem is basically one of legitimizing corporate power. The authors, in exploring the possible ways to reestablish public trust in business, consider the classical and managerial creeds as descriptions of corporate responsibility and find both insufficient in that, while the first is too narrow in its concerns and adequate only for small business, the second, though broader, still reflects only the business perspective. Neither express the concerns of the public. Rather, the authors suggest a public consent creed derived from the Lockean notion that government is always subject to public consent. They point out that, obviously, only an analogy applies between government and business in regard to consent because we vote for the former but not for the latter. Business must be responsive to public interests but they don't say much more about the analogy which allows application of the consent creed. Just how must business be responsible to public interests? Must business give priority to public interests in carrying on their practice? That sounds like a formula for ruining any business. Perhaps some kinds of business are more readily tuned to public concern than others and certainly an established company can support some community interests without results detrimental to the business. But that is not so for many kinds of business and sometimes less so than others. On what is the analogy with the consent creed based? Two chapters later, in connection with business corruption and sharp practice, the authors suggest that what is needed is for corporate leaders to be deeply moral and for them to lay down and "inspect for compliance" moral codes for practice in their companies.[17] I think the grounds for the analogy with the consent creed lie in this suggestion but nowhere do the authors make it clear. However, the authors make the problem clear for the business community in the way no other book I know of does. Let me quote a relevant paragraph:

> A business community, if it is to assume a position of leadership in society, must somehow generate a vision of purpose that transcends its own role and its own direct and immediate benefits. But such a transcendent vision is extremely difficult for American businessmen to attain, since it appears to conflict with the traditional and deepest American ideology, to which Alexis de Tocqueville, a century and a half ago, gave the name 'the philosophy of self-interest.' Today, as when the Republic was still young, Americans generally deny that they ever behave altruistically. In this respect, Tocqueville said that Americans often failed to do justice to themselves; although he found that the Americans, like people everywhere, sometimes give way to 'those disinterested and spontaneous impulses that are natural to man', he said that Americans seldom would 'admit that they yield to emotions of this kind; they are more anxious to do honor to their philosophy than to themselves.'[18]

What this means is that we practice better than we think, at least sometimes. The authors go on to point out that traditional ideology inhibits the businessman because it is "too narrowly *economic*". Whether this means that something other than the economic should be taken into account or that the economics, as economics, of our tradition is too narrow is not clear. In a search for a solution to the problem of legitimacy, of restoring public trust in business, I believe both alternatives to be involved.

The doctrine of self-interest, as previously pointed out, is ambiguous. At its narrowest it means the individual is ultimately concerned about himself. This is selfishness and almost everyone is against outright selfishness on moral grounds. Very often business practice, with its emphasis on bottom line profit, fits nicely under this version. Some of the moral curse is taken off of this narrowest version of self-interest when it is modified from direct self-concern to indirect self-concern. It is called enlightened self-interest—in order to get what I need I must give someone else what they need. It has never been shown either (a) that all individual concern is simply selfish, in the way assumed by all narrow versions of self-interest, or (b) that some other-regarding motive, needed to make sense out of the seemingly self-sacrificial behavior of parents toward their children or soldiers toward their buddies, is really included as part of that concern. That something on the order of the second alternative (b) is the case I have no empirical reasons to doubt, but, in any case, altruism, if possible, would not advance a solution to our problem at all. It remains as it is: either be altruistic or run my business properly.

We must find some way of relating self-regarding and other-regarding interests in the logically weak sense of "either-or and possibly both" instead of the mutually exclusive sense of "either-or and not possibly both" as our tradition would have it. I expect the use of the exclusive sense is attributable to our modern concern for the uniqueness of the self on analogy with the atomism underlying Newtonian mechanics. Certainly, many interests are unique and perhaps some interests, like property, are weakened when shared, but any reflection upon self-interest which fails to show that it is dependent upon certain conditions for support is clearly inadequate, an individualism with its head cut off.

The conception of these enabling conditions being developed here fits that requirement quite well. No matter what the interests of business may be and surely profit will be part of it, there is one thing they should be interested in, the conditions supporting self-interest as a mode of behavior. These are the same conditions that support responsible public consent and should be of interest to all persons in the community. The morality of enabling conditions advanced here sets out the limiting conditions within which any object of interest or means of practice will be consistent with its own possibility and not undercut the well-being of the agent and at the same time assures the support of those conditions of practice for every one else. Such a conception of morality falls within the public consent creed in that trustworthiness on the part of business tends to engender consent on the part of the public. And they willingly not only purchase the product, which the classical creed considered sufficient, but do so in the expectation of being treated fairly and like human beings in the transaction. In one sense, the classical creed was correct in the idea that its duty to the public was fulfilled in producing a good product at a reasonable price. But under present conditions of hugh corporate operations much more than product and price are included in their responsibilities. The moral conception suggested here fulfills one of the considerations implied by the phrase "social responsibility." The other side of that phrase refers to what support an individual business can voluntarily give to particular community problems from the local to the national and even the international level, but always within the criteria of what is consistent with its own possibility. Just how this can sensibly be done is a function of the condition of each business, the nature of its product and its operation, and the recognition of its own dependence upon the larger community. Business, as well as governmental, practice presupposes these enabling conditions and the awareness and formulation of them as best we can would go a long way toward bringing about the conditions for a workable relationship between business and the public, but also, as proposed by Silk and Vogel, between business and government as the peoples' representative.

Now, let me draw together the strands from considering these three contemporary studies of individualism. *Habits of the Heart* put the matter in terms of commitment to something other than the self. On the surface, this appears to conflict with our self-interested conception of the human. *Individualism and Public Life* put the matter in terms of the need for a disinterested concern for the public good on the part of the individual. This also seems to conflict with self-interest but brings forward the conception of reason. *Ethics and Profits* suggested a consent creed, a principle part of which would be moral practice by individual firms but left untouched how the consent creed and moral practice are related.

All three consider individualism based on self-interest alone to be unsatisfactory. It is clear that this modern and unsatisfactory individualism has been with us, at least in principle, since Locke and the Founding Fathers. Why has its unsatisfactoriness only become obvious two hundred years later? I suspect it is because during that period of time faith in its principle of commitment, reason, has eroded. Reason, as the instrument of universal truth was the way out of self-interested individualism. As assurance of that principle of commitment began to erode under Hume's critique of causality, the sensationalism that unaided empiricism leads to, the implications of evolution for our understanding of change in all our sciences and the coming of a process orientation towards reality, the nakedness of this version of individualism begins to show in the problems these three books look into. When reason is no longer considered as being able to deliver the theoretical truth as anchor for our commitment beyond ourselves, atomistic individualism is in trouble. To say, with the Pragmatists for example, that our knowledge is always incomplete and a matter of development through experience preserves the usages of scientific reason but is of very little help in moral judgment where we are concerned not to make a wrong judgment prior to any testing in experience. The absoluteness of our moral values was the last to be affected by these changes. As faith in reason fades we have buttressed these moral certainties by religious faith or by feeling or, as my students, under the pressure of their need for standards as well as their beliefs that everyone is unique and all values relative, frequently qualify historic meaning and usage and say "Right, for me." The same shoring-up is evident in the transformation of the realm of theoretical knowing in the social sciences into the realm of ideology where the values are built into the theoretical assumptions with no concern for truth expressed at all; truth, instead of getting you out there, only makes sense within a given system, such as democratic capitalism or Euclidean geometry. As a result our values are seen as subjective, relative and private, and, as we read everyday, there is less and less foundation for a sense of community to hold us together. The jungle conditions of our inner cities are the everyday counterpart of this way of thinking or should I say lack of thinking.

In the light of these results perhaps it was wrong-headed to begin with to associate the theoretical use of reason with the delivery of truth. There is a long history of their association going back at least to Aristotle for whom theoretical reason is separated from and given priority over practical reason. Plato is often understood in the same way and yet I am not at all sure that this basic separation is to be found in Plato. The reflective use of reason employed to establish awareness of the enabling conditions as the foundation for responsible practice will have to be looked into further but, at present, our concern is with these conditions as the ground for moral values.

We have been putting up with individual persons who are not aware of these moral conditions because only rarely can the individual by himself do much harm, and as I said, most of us practice better than we think. We have put up with businesses that show in their practice no awareness of these moral conditions because in many ways over the years, so the argument goes, they have improved our level of living, but at an awful cost to some. Lately, we have empowered our government to regulate the practices of business in our name because we lack the power ourselves and, while much progress has been made, we find that our governors themselves are, by and large, no better off than business as far as these moral conditions are concerned. So business and government do not trust each other and the public, quite justifiably, doesn't trust either of them. We, ourselves, may not be explicitly aware of those moral conditions enabling our practice either but we have sense enough to know very often when something isn't right; for instance, we know, as Silk and Vogel make clear, that we don't mind if someone makes a profit as long as a service is being rendered but we hate being taken advantage of by anyone for any reason; we also know that the 1988 presidential campaign was an insult to our whole way of life. We were being treated like bundles of narrow gauge self-interest and the candidates pander to these supposedly preferential interests instead of speaking to our common concerns. It is just another instance of our thinking about ourselves being inadequate to the facts about ourselves. It seems to get worse every year — a self-fulfilling prophecy destroying its own possibility, our democratic way of life.

A look at our history shows that we have done many things right and that we still exist as a nation and as a free people because of them. Maybe, as some will say, more than anything else we have been lucky and they have a point. But that is yesterday, and my concern is with tomorrow.

Individualism means pluralism and we hear much about that. Individualism, in the narrow sense in which we have been speaking of it, also means relativism. Relativism, in the framework of this narrow individualism, means that all value judgments and even all knowledge and opinions, with their built-in bias, are merely individual, personal, of the moment and trivia, unless backed by power. Unless we come to realize that the very pluralism and relativism of values which we think can enrich and deepen our individualism require some enabling conditions common to the whole enterprize of individualism and without which that enterprise will self-destruct—unless we begin to take them seriously in our practice, we are attending our own funeral. I cannot put why I think these enabling conditions are important in any stronger terms than that.

Footnotes

1. Berkeley: University of California Press, 1985; Perennial Library, Harper & Row, 1986. Hereafter, HH.

2. HH, pp. 28-35.

3. HH, p. 143.

4. Ibid.

5. New York: Basil Blackwell Inc., 1987. Hereafter, IPL.

6. IPL, p. x-xi, bracketed material added by JW.

7. IPL, p. 67-8.

8. IPL, p. 69-70.

9. IPL, p. 164.

10. IPL, p. 174-5.

11. IPL, p. 184

12. IPL, p. 185.

13. IPL, p. 214.

14. IPL, p. 208.

15. IPL, p. 209.

16. IPL, p. 211.

17. E&P, pp.225-6.

18. E&P, p.233.

The Enabling Conditions: Applications II

CHAPTER 5

Continuing to emphasize the importance of the enabling conditions, this chapter will be devoted to sketching out their application to four differing but related areas, rights, contract, the free market and the idea of regulation.

This application will serve at least to relate these enabling conditions to areas closely connected to business practice and to indicate a line of development from these most general principles to the less abstract concerns of business practice. And since these four areas are closely tied in practice to our legal structures, the relationship between law and morality as conceived here will become evident.

From our perspective of an ethic of practice, the notion of rights is a modern conception, the advent and development of which coincides with the modern emphasis upon the ultimate value of the individual. In its early uses, rights were instruments of protection for the individual citizen not only from his fellow citizens but, primarily, against the powers exercised by the rulers of the newly-formed nation-states. One of the most interesting problems arising with this notion of rights has to do with the equally important notion of obligations or duties, and responsibility is one of the strands being looked into in this work. In medieval times rights and duties were derived from, and operationally helped to define, the status of the individual as a member of a class in the hierarchical social order. With the break-up of this originally Oriental notion of empire with its hierarchically ordered system, first in the Protestant reformation and the coming of nationalism and then in the French Revolution with its reverberations throughout the whole European world, the emphasis on individual rights came to be dominant and individual duties came to be a kind of poor relation, in that the rights of a person imply the duties of all other persons in respect to those rights; in short, rights became primary. It is understandable how this imbalance between rights and duties should come about. In keeping with the contemporaneous emphasis upon freedom and equality, rights tend to take the form of common human needs and interests or claims (at law). It is the total absence of any ground for obligation in the utility principle mentioned in Chapter three, that if everyone pursues his self-interest the good of the community will be promoted, that raises the question about the relation of self-interest to the public good. In our own time, our own individualism in the United States has been so preoccupied with individual rights that our sense of community has deteriorated dangerously. And the ideal of the great, centralized society as an adequate substitute for a community of reciprocally related and practicing individuals has come up very short in the balance needed between rights and duties, and badly undercuts, in many areas, the self-disciplining element so essential to free, responsible, and creatively productive individual practice. It has become a perversion of traditional and classical liberalism. With his usual insightfulness, R.H.Tawney, in *The Acquisitive Society*, defines a privilege as a right for which there is no corresponding function.[1] Consistent with an ethic of practice, it should be emphasized that the constraint or obligation corresponding to the right is implicit for reflection within the context of practicing that right or any other; my right to swing my fist stops where my duty and your right begins, at your nose. In Chapter Two the characteristics describing practice were laid out and, lest we forget, #12 says that

> Business practice requires the distinction between the ideal and the real. Errors occur and ideally they should not. Practice must recognize the difference between what is and what ought to be.

In that distinctively human behavior called practice not everything is permitted—only what is consistent with its own possibility, with the maintenance and continuation of the distinctively human. Responsible practice presupposes certain capacities in the individual and it is the maintenance and protection of these capacities with which rights are concerned. These capacities can be called God-given, if you wish, but they need exercise, development, education, sensitivity, habituation, self-discipline and outside support in order to flower and they can result, in varying degrees through the practice of individuals and communities, in the general level of civilization as we know it and in the creativity of the human spirit for both good and evil. To encourage the former and constrain the latter is both the function as well as the justification of the notion of rights.

As we have discovered in our own civil rights experience, such rights, to be efficacious, must be anchored as well as expressed in three ways; in real possibilities in human nature and social relationships, in our awareness of them as capacities beneficial to the individual and the community, and in our founding documents and the laws which supplement them.

Under the first of the three, for example, the right to knowledge, i.e., to be educated or to be informed about products to be used or consumed, would have no foundation at all if the truth about any state or condition is both relative and subjective. Common usage would agree with this notion as regards facts and the descriptions of things factually but would have doubts about its application to values. It should be clear, however, that the facts about "cholesterol free" margarine or "sugar free" soda function as values in my concern as shopper for the well-being of my cardiovascular system or my teeth. It is an erroneous notion that fact is basic. As has been argued here, it is practice that is basic and what is considered to be fact comes to be so considered only as a result of practice and even, in large part, for the sake of practice. For practice as activity embodies both structure (fact) and its limitations as criteria (value) for choice in its purposiveness. True, the value placed on facts may differ for individuals, some shoppers may not care about their cardiovascular systems or their teeth. Considering what is known about such matters, we may judge such shoppers as foolish or shortsighted and such value judgment is by no means subjective although it is relative to the state of our knowledge about these matters.

And the same considerations can be extended in the same way to the capacities in humans encouraging and supporting human practice as we conceive it, that is, those capacities to be free (to initiate action and to make choices), to be concerned (to care not only for the maintenance of these capacities as well as the pursuit of chosen ends but a prudent concern for the risks and uncertainties inevitably connected with practice in this world), and to be consistent (to keep ones practice free from both logical and pragmatic inconsistency). These are the real possibilities in human nature on which rights must be grounded.

Under the second of the three, our awareness of these rights as beneficial to individuals and the community, responsible practice is critical,[2] that is, it is carried on in the light of criteria not only for success with some sought after goal but success in the preservation of the ability to practice. These rights need conceptualization as criteria as well as specification in the many and differing applications and limitations which experience will introduce. Some sense of their meaning and applicability must be developed or they soon become useless baggage. They may even be taken for granted as criteria in practice but should be subject to recall and examination should occasion arise.

Under the third, these rights must be stated in simple, ideal form in our basic documents and then, as our experience brings to light particular applications and limitations relevant to our practice, they receive more concrete expression in our laws. The latter is a never-ending job for bad law cripples responsible practice. The adjustment of a legal system to the demands of responsible practice is never complete. It cannot be and this is where the distinction between law and morality arises. The principles used in judging the adequacy of existing law are often referred to as a "higher law" and always in moral terms as "right" as opposed to the "wrong" of the law in question. In our terms, however, such principles often represent clearer insight into the enabling conditions of adequate human practice in the areas covered by the law in question. It is essential to realize that law is an abstract structure of meanings designed to optimize and regulate the conditions of practice of the citizenry. Perhaps, we normally think of the law in negative terms as forbidding certain practices, but the law, like all structures of meaning, also has a positive and enabling function, for example, the idea of just practice, as well as a negative, restrictive function, for example, the ideas of collusion, misrepresentation and harm or damage. By restricting the conditions of practice in certain ways, the limits on just practice are worked out and these limitations ultimately constitute our operational conception of just practice at law. Changing conditions, of course, require adjustments. Many times our operating legal system expresses our moral insights very well indeed. But sometimes it does not and correction is needed. It is just here that the position of the businessman who believes all he has to do is be profitable and stay within the law can be seen as irresponsible. To put the matter simply, the businessman is also a citizen and being concerned about the structure of his own practice is of first importance for his business. These considerations underlie the argument against excessive government regulation advanced at The Conference Board meetings discussed in Silk and Vogel's *Ethics and Profits*, previously cited. The argument was that existing regulation precluded the possibility of responsible practice by the business community. This is a serious objection because, to the degree that it is well-founded, it bears out our previous observation about the slow change from a market to a command economy embodied in our recent history and the gradual undercutting of our democratic practice. The emphasis upon the enabling conditions here is to point up that nothing in our system can take the place of individual, self-disciplined practice. Government can encourage and support responsible practice but government cannot take the place of responsible practice without undercutting its possibility. These are complex and difficult matters but they are part of the price of the self-government required by responsible freedom. It should be clear from the above that our concern here is with moral rights and not with legal rights except for illustration.

The foundation, then, for a theory of rights, no matter how we choose to delineate what in fact such rights might be, would rest upon those enabling conditions without which responsible practice is impossible and would be designed to maintain those capacities of the individual the exercise of which may produce responsible practice.

In moving towards the determination of the moral rights expressing these capacities, suppose we say that everyone has a right to practice responsibly. Is that right absolute? In keeping with the bi-polarity of practice, the Self or inner pole and the World or outer pole require differing but related perspectives both of which are included in our understanding of any and all rights. When we consider the Self or inner pole in abstraction from the rest of practice, rights receive their most absolute and ideal formulation. But in practice individual action is always subject to limitation. Such limitations arise in several ways and we take them into our understanding of rights. For example, the freedom of speech of an individual is morally limited at law by Justice Holmes' doctrine of "clear and present danger." Shouting "Fire" in a crowded building when there is no fire would significantly alter the conditions of practice for everyone to the detriment of their abilities to practice responsibly. In this case the security of the enabling conditions is undercut from inside the context of practice. In a second way, when we are at war, conditions of practice are prudently restricted to meet the external threat to them. In a third and much more complex way, while we want individuals to exercise their capacities responsibly and to the fullest extent compatible with existing conditions, we recognize that some individuals lack these capacities in some degree, such as children, the elderly and the ill, and we place appropriate limitations on their practice both for their benefit and the benefit of everyone else.

The forgoing examples indicate that while some rights are more basic than others there are none that are not subject to limitations under certain conditions. Consideration of the distinction between positive and negative rights, one that is basic to rights theory, should give us further insight into the nature and status of rights. To do this, however, it would be best to return to the historical perspective used earlier in the chapter.

Early rights theory, for example, that of John Locke (1632-1704) with his rights to "life, liberty and property," is usually characterized as negative in form—the life, liberty and property of an individual are not to be interfered with by government or other persons. Our Bill of Rights in the Constitution has this negative function. We took the same negative orientation to the enabling conditions in relation to the threat posed to them by freedom of choice. More recent statements of rights, for example, the "Universal Declaration of Human Rights" of the United Nations contains positive rights as well. In positive form a right names some thing or condition that will be provided for and can be expected by the individual; work, education, health care, social security and the whole set of entitlements against the community at large associated with the welfare state are examples. The logic of this development from negative to positive rights is impressive. How are you to practice responsibly if there is no work or if you are ignorant or in poor health? Doesn't the maintenance of those capacities of the individual involve at least a minimum set of positive conditions without which the capacities maintained by negative rights have little chance of responsible exercise? The problem becomes one of where do you draw the line or what aspects of an individual's condition you are going to leave up to the individual. The classic advice in recognition of this problem is that we shouldn't provide the fish for people to eat we should teach them how to fish. That may work well as long as there are enough fish to catch but you may wind up having to support the fish supply. An interesting version of this same dilemma is under consideration presently.

With so many sources of individual income being handled by direct deposit in banks these days, for example, social security and pensions, wouldn't it be a good idea to have banks supply free individual checking accounts to the less fortunate members of our society? Such a right would work at least two benefits. It would encourage everyone to behave more responsibly in handling their economic affairs. It would also keep as many people as possible participating in our consumer oriented economy. Of course, someone would have to pay the cost of this and it might well be less expensive in the long run for the bank's customers to pay the cost than if it went through Washington in the form of government support. In either case workable cut-off limits would need to be worked out to eliminate those who have made good use of the opportunity given them to participate and no longer qualify. In general, it seems that very few governmental programs designed to ameliorate an undesirable condition — and I am thinking specifically of what is called "reverse discrimination" designed to reestablish a balance disturbed by historical and still present discrimination against minorities, — very few contain any temporal limitations indicating that such leaning in the other direction is a temporary condition to be discontinued as the need decreases. An objection will be that prejudice will always be with us but, while this may be true, if the program achieves its goal, then non-discriminatory hiring practices may be so widely adopted that the conditions of individual justice may be restored. Welfare programs are difficult to administer and are sometimes self-defeating. In one sense, the welfare state fully maintains the conditions for the exercise of responsible practice but, in another sense, by doing so it undercuts the significance of responsible practice itself. Self-fulfillment is always in response to a challenge and welfare, while it may make the challenge more manageable, may also remove the challenge. In so far as this is so, self-government will have been destroyed. But because the efficacy of negative rights presuppose some positive rights such as education, certainly among the earliest positive rights to be recognized, does not mean they must be supplied by the national community alone. Much has been and could be done on the local levels and, where feasible, something should be required of the recipients in the way of payment. In emergency situations such aid should be given until people get on their feet again, but one wonders about such support as permanent for the reasons just given. The case of the small family farm during my whole lifetime is a classic example and a complicated one. I think a case can be made that such small farms as part of our industrial nation have been in a state of perpetual emergency for the entire 20th Century because they, as units, cannot continue to exist on the outskirts of an industrial civilization for reasons advanced by Adam Smith in the sections on the division of labor at the beginning of his *Wealth of Nations*. The level of wealth produced by industry both lures the farmer to a better life off the farm and drives him from the farm as unable to compete with his industrial neighbors. Unfortunately, this demise of the small farm contributes to weakening the conditions of self-sufficiency and independence for the individual as well as the family. At any rate, all these changes affect the conditions of, and hence the limitations on, individual practice and that is the point.

All of the various limitations on rights suggested above qualify practice from the point of view of the World-pole of practice through the three external conditions, multiplicity, continuity, and structure. Now let us turn to the Self-pole and consider its relationship to the enabling conditions and to their expression in terms of rights.

Basically, there is no better statement of this relationship that I know of than that by Norman Bowie and Simon L. Simon:

> Rights, we are suggesting, are fundamental moral commodities because they enable us to stand up on our own two feet, "to look others in the eye," and to feel in some fundamental way the equal of anyone. To think of oneself as the holder of rights is not to be unduly but properly proud, to have that minimal self-respect that is necessary to be worthy of the love and esteem of others. Conversely, to lack the concept of oneself as a rights bearer is to be bereft of a significant element of human dignity. Without such a concept, we could not view ourselves as beings entitled to be treated as not simply means but ends as well.[3]

The Self is a "rights holder" and such rights are expressed as "self-respect," "dignity" and "treated as not simply means but ends as well." The last sentence of the above quote, it should be noted, reflects Kant's third formulation of the categorical imperative (p. 32). To these can be added autonomy, equal consideration and freedom. All, however, reflect the Self as capable of responsible practice in terms of the three conditions, choice, concern and consistency. There are other ways of expressing these rights as well but all of them reflect differing aspects, some more basic and some derivative, of the responsible practice of the individual that enables such practice.

Even though there is much controversy over just which rights are most basic, there is general agreement that those that are basic rights are moral, that is, they are universal, apply equally to all humans and ought to be respected. As yet, the obligatoriness of the moral "ought" has not been discussed here, but in setting forth the enabling conditions of practice it was pointed out that they are common to all who practice, that they apply equally to each who practices and that the relation of those enabling conditions to practice constitutes the moral dimension for humans. Their obligatoriness, however, is of first concern and will be taken up in Chapter Eight.

If there is one special area of rights which clearly and without doubt concerns itself with practice and its enabling conditions it is the theory of contracts in law. It is often pointed out that while much of medieval law was based on status, much of modern law is based upon the idea of contract which assumes freedom, individualism, change and progress. Contract presupposes freedom of choice and the capacities to practice responsibly. In a contract there is a mutual, reciprocal agreement to practice in certain specified ways by two or more persons. The guiding ideas in contract are moral in that promises are made which ought to be kept or measures of redress take hold. It is assumed that all relevant conditions are known by the parties to the contract and that each party is capable of holding up his end and intends to do so. The law, of course, can not read a person's intentions but the contractual form, the agreement, the measures of redress and the "consideration" involved are taken as inducements as well as indications of sincerity. The contract is the form for responsible practicing between persons where a mutual exchange is involved. There are some indications that we are swinging back to a status base again in that society grows more structured as minority rights and economic considerations become more prominent. But even these status concerns like those contained in the individual agreements in contract point to the conditions enabling individual practice in a just manner. The idea of contract presupposes the enabling conditions of practice and exhibits all of the characteristics attributable to practice in our earlier chapters. That the idea of contract is ubiquitous throughout our society goes without saying. On analogy with this basis for contract theory, the contractarian view of the origins of the political state can be understood as founded upon these same considerations concerning practice and the moral.

Now, with the enabling conditions of practice understood in terms of human rights and the idea of contract as expressing and protecting the conditions of reciprocally just practice by individuals, let us turn to the idea of the "free market" and its relation to these enabling conditions. Often the phrase "free market" is spoken of and used as if there were no limitations connected with it at all; much the way we use the phrase "it's a free country, isn't it?" This is one of the two meanings of freedom that are part and parcel of our Western tradition. On this view, an individual is free if there is no outside interference, if one can do as one wishes. It is this idea of freedom that finds expression in Nietzsche's (in)famous saying "If God is dead, then everything is permitted." There is nothing stopping an individual with a free will from doing as he wishes and the rightness or wrongness, the moral character, of any action has reference only to the fulfilling of those wishes. This is the rugged individualism spoken of in the Preface and it often appears that it is the condition operating in the "free market," a system in which an aggregation of self-interested, profit maximizing, individuals compete with each other in a zero-sum game of king of the hill.

There is also another idea of freedom in our tradition as set forth in the early chapters here. This idea agrees that individual freedom precludes outside interference but it goes on to point out that because an act of free choice in the seeking to do as one wishes can limit and even destroy the very conditions that make such acts possible, the individual is not free in any dynamic and continuing way unless the acts of ones freedom, although directed towards what one wants, are consistent with their own possibility. Then the individual is free, self-governing and responsible because, as we have said, the conditions which enable the individual to be a person are the same for all individuals.

But, even though much of the talk about the "free market" is based on the first notion of freedom given above, most every introductory economics text recognizes that there are certain conditions necessary for the free market to come about. They are usually set forth in connection with the ideal of perfect competition which is understood as a model that never was on land or sea but a model that allows us to understand the values of competition and the desirability of keeping markets as competitive as possible. The first such value is that the free market can allocate and distribute goods and resources more efficiently than any other arrangement and the second value is that the free market allows a maximum of individual freedom. Our concern here is with the second such value and over the years the argument that the free market in our country is one of the major supports of the freedom in our democratic way of life has been both consistent and important.[4] Our questions become: "Which sense of freedom is native to the free market?" and "What are the characteristics of perfectly competitive free markets?" Let us consider the latter question first. (In the following discussion the characteristics given are to be found in Professor Manuel Velasquez's book, *Business Ethics: Concepts and Cases*.[5] Professor Velasquez presents seven features of the free market:

1. There are numerous buyers and many sellers, none of whom has a substantial share of the market.
2. All buyers and sellers can freely and immediately enter or leave the market.

> 3. Every buyer and seller has full and perfect knowledge of what every other buyer and seller is doing, including knowledge of the prices, quantities, and qualities of all goods being bought and sold.
> 4. The goods being sold in the market are so similar to each other that no one cares from whom each buys or sells.
> 5. The costs and benefits of producing or using the goods being exchanged are borne entirely by those buying or selling the goods and not by any other external parties.
> 6. All buyers and sellers are utility maximizers: each tries to get as much as possible for as little as possible.
> 7. No external parties (such as the government) regulate the price, quantity, or quality of any of the goods being bought and sold in the market.

Velasquez goes on to say:

> In addition to these seven characteristics, free competitive markets also need an enforceable private property system (otherwise buyers and sellers would not have any "ownership rights" to exchange), an underlying system of contracts (which allows buyers and sellers to forge agreements that transfer ownership), and an underlying system of production (that generates goods or services whose ownership can be exchanged).[6]

There are several things that need to be said about these seven conditions, not in criticism but to clarify what is being talked about. In the first place, these conditions apply to each different commodity being traded so that there would be a free market in bread and in shoes and in bicycles, for example. This is the only way to make sense out of condition four in context with the rest. Secondly, buyers and sellers are practicing individuals trading under the contractual conditions discussed previously and moved to trade for any given commodity by their desire for it coupled with the desire neither to pay more than they have to for it as buyer nor take less than they have to for it as seller, as the case may be. There are many buyers and sellers in each market and there are no "better mousetraps" in any of the markets.

Now, the practice of buyers and sellers presupposes the enabling conditions of practice as set forth in Chapter Two. These conditions are as much a part of free market practice as they are of any kind of purposive activity. They constitute a set of internal constraints upon market practice, without which, no market practice, and they are in addition to the seven conditions just set forth for a free market. In short, the second idea of freedom as outlined previously is required by the free market as well as the first, freedom from outside interference. Too much economic thought, in marking out the conditions for the free market, refers only to the first sense of freedom. Characteristic seven does this above. But then, how are these seven conditions and the enabling conditions of practice to be maintained in the free market situation? This is an important question because, as trading in a commodity goes on, some will compete more successfully than others for reasons of a better product, lower costs or better service and, as successful, the market is tipped in their favor; losers get into something else at best and winners increase their staying power in the market. So, what maintains the conditions of the practicing, free market to the highest degree possible? Of the three added conditions, private property, a system of contracts and a system of production, the last offers nothing in support. If, however, the first, private property, be taken in the widest sense, as in the Allgeyer case, (p.5), to include ones life and capacities, then it becomes an extension of ones individual rights as capacities to be enabled by morality and law. The second, a system of contracts, embodies these enabling conditions, as we have previously shown, since it deals with the nature of the activity in the market. Adam Smith was worried about the effects of success upon the market in terms of monopoly as destructive of free market conditions. The idea of limitations upon the free market has been present from the start. But generally it has been left more and more to government as the most appropriate institution to do the job. Individuals are, by definition, too busy trading. Historically, of course, our first regulatory actions on these lines were the Sherman Anti-Trust and the Clayton Acts. But to leave it to government is to introduce external interference and by degrees to replace the market with a command economy. In market language, the citizens as buyers have been protecting their health, their environment and their capacities to practice responsibly from the effects, intended or otherwise, wrought by citizens as sellers upon the conditions of practice in their attempts to compete successfully in the market place. Of course, most of us as practicing individuals function as both buyers and sellers in many markets. It is no wonder that the community of sellers, the businessmen, feels the pressure. The conditions of market equilibrium have been violently disrupted.

Back in the early days of market theory when businesses were many and small, only monopolization of the market would destroy the conditions of freedom and competition. The comings and goings of individual losers would have no effect since it was assumed they entered other markets. Only the consistent winners were a problem for market conditions. But with the coming of factories, industry and the growth of large corporations something else besides monopoly affects free market conditions, the occurrence of corporate failure. Not every corporate failure but large corporate failure affects the system. As example, consider the Chrysler case.

Chrysler Corporation, you will remember, asked Government for a loan to stave-off insolvency. From one perspective, such a loan looked like totally unjustified external interference with the market system. Along with the possibility of competitive success goes the risk of competitive failure and support favoring one member is not only unfair to other market members but destructive of free market conditions. I am not for a moment suggesting that whether Chrysler was a good financial risk isn't the first consideration in the use of public funds but the argument that outside interference damages the free market system can be turned around 180°. Considering the size and degree of involvement of Chrysler in the automotive market and all the markets subsidiary to the automotive in one way or another, it should be argued that the damage to the market would be far greater if the Government failed to give Chrysler the loan than if it did. The dislocations in our economy made by Chrysler's failure measured in terms of jobs, taxes, purchasing power, unemployment benefits and pension funds over the period of time needed for the market to make use of what would remain of Chrysler in people and things add up to a weakening of the economy unless large amounts of public money would be used to offset such dislocations. If the function of government is to insure as best it can the conditions of responsible practice for its citizenry, then, given a reasonable chance for success, the loan should be granted as consistent with the function of government. This case is one instance where treating a corporation as if it is just another person in the market runs into trouble. Clearly where failure is concerned, Chrysler is just a gathering tank for the interests and capacities of the persons who act for it and interact with it. Corporate failure in the market is not like individual failure in the market and the differences are a function, at least in part, of the degree of size. In these matters corporations are at best second-class persons. Bankruptcy dissolves the corporate person into its dependencies, its oneness into its manyness. And how large a corporation must be before such dissolution threatens the economy itself is a good question and beyond us here. But the point of the case for us was that the conditions of failure as well as of success are a threat to the seven conditions of the free market with which we are concerned. Further, the analysis presented was designed to emphasize that the theory of free market practice if based only on the first idea of freedom and leaving the supporting conditions of that market to be maintained by government will slowly undercut and destroy its own possibility. I think we have been watching this happen. I am not in any way implying that regulation by government is a mistake. Far from it! The mistake lies in supposing that external regulation of any kind can do the job where that regulation is not an expression of something the people living under the regulation agree ought to be done. I recall the ineffectiveness of the 18th Amendment for that very reason and our experience with civil rights, while expressed in laws, centers in the second condition mentioned previously, the awareness by the individual of the need as well as the moral obligation to maintain the enabling conditions of his own practice as well as everyone elses. The first type of freedom is commonly known as license and our democratic way, economic, political or individual, cannot survive in terms of it alone. The conception of self-government requires the second type of freedom and is as important for the free market system as it is for the political system because both depend upon the self-governing, responsible individual for their continuation. Nothing less will do the job.

In my remarks on the market system the topic of regulation came up in connection with freedom. As might be expected from earlier comments, the topic of regulation poses the severest challenge to the analogy between the individual and the corporation that we have been making use of. As the final example of the application of the enabling conditions of practice, I want to consider the nature of regulation.

In bringing up our children we cannot produce responsible behavior without extending them the freedom to exercise critical choice. High-handed regulation of our children's behavior can preclude the possibility of their ever being really responsible. This is no apology for a standardless permissiveness, just recognition that in matters of regulation the community can throw the baby out with the bath water. The power to regulate is the power to destroy and we must regulate so as to allow the freedom and autonomy needed for responsible activity. And this is where the shoe pinches, for the very possibility of responsible practice by a person includes the possibility of irresponsible action; the moral includes the immoral within it as a possibility. Considering the power and influence which business exerts upon society this is not a prospect to be viewed lightly. And yet I see no complete remedy from the outside for this risk without slowly but surely reducing the areas in which purposive activity as spoken of here will even be possible. Again, this is not an apology for corporate freedom. Much regulation, enabling as well as restricting and prohibiting, is both possible and desirable, but the capacity to be an end-in-itself, a person, must not be removed or else the conditions of practice by responsible persons will be severely crippled in our society. This is one respect in which the analogy between persons and corporations holds good and merits our concern. It is for this reason that many businesses are trying to be self-governing and set standards of their own. At the same time the orientation of business trade books has changed basically in keeping with the emphasis upon knowledge users that has come to the forefront. John Naisbitt and Patricia Aburdene in their *Reinventing the Corporation* express this change:

> In an industrial society, the strategic resource is capital. In the new information society, that key resource has shifted to information, knowledge, creativity. And there is only one place where the corporation can mine this valuable new resource—in its employees. That means a whole new emphasis on human resources.[7]

Only individuals can handle information and the conditions, external and internal, of those individuals equipped to handle information have become of primary concern. This entrepreneurial orientation is essentially self-governing and is based upon the values and perspective with which we are concerned here. There are different ways, or levels at which, to regulate and we should look at them briefly to indicate the application of our analysis of practice.

The surest way of regulating the flow of traffic across the front yard is to fence it in. If the threat is from small children, unruly mobs, or any and all free-wandering animals, you may have to do just that. However, if the threat is from the comings and goings of individuals in daily commerce, signs saying "Keep of the grass" located strategically may well do the job. But notice this form of regulation presupposes something about the regulated other than the capacity to move around. It requires the ability to read and understand the sign as well as the capacity to see the meaning as applying to the person reading the sign, "this means me," and the ability to direct my movements in conformity with the message. This type of regulation, simple as it is, requires purposive activity on the part of the regulated to carry it out. The very same assumptions are in force with laws and regulations, except that the problem is more difficult. Because the conditions stipulated in laws and regulations are general in nature and because those being regulated are always in some particular situation, a judgment must be made that this situation comes under this regulation and not some other. This requires choice and critical activity. You can regulate by requiring that certain things be taken into account (pollution) or not be taken into account (race, color or creed) in the decision process and the ensuing activities. This narrows the available options, puts uninteresting consequences behind non-compliance and sharpens the sensibilities of those involved. And as long as such regulation doesn't get on the other side of what are "reasonable" operating conditions in a given industry or situation, regulation and responsibility can go hand in hand. Historically speaking, most of our regulation by the community at whatever level springs from the desire to rule out certain abuses. This is largely a negative affair and can become stifling. But if you value the activity involved then your regulation, like the rules in any game, must strike a balance that enables as well as limits. I suspect the truth of this observation is exemplified in our current attempts to "deregulate" the transportation industry, air, train and truck. It is worth noting in passing that this is the main function of a Bill of Rights, to balance the positive powers given to government in the Constitution, which act negatively upon individuals, with some enabling powers of their own. The point about regulation can be put in another way: Is the public interest so all inclusive that there is no room for private interest? But perhaps one of the most basic public interests is exactly the preservation of the enabling conditions of private interest.

The degree to which this point is affirmed is the degree to which the problem of regulation has a large dimension of education within it. We often think we lay down the conditions for responsible practice by just leaving the room needed for such and we are often tragically disappointed by our children, by our cities (where the pressures against civilized behavior appear to increase daily) and even by our government. We seem to be learning, however, that we have to get inside the decision activity of our institutions, not to dictate restrictions so much as to instill sensitivity to the basic values and conditions that permit responsibility and the freedom that goes with it for everyone.

It was mentioned previously that many corporations in order to protect themselves from the threat or possibility of outside regulation have developed codes of ethics to cover procedures in their various operational areas. No doubt it is under similar outside pressures that the codes which all the traditional professions possess developed. In the second paragraph of the oldest such code that we know, the Oath of Hippocrates, the concern is to protect the "precepts and oral instruction and other learning" from possession and abuse by others not under the oath. In our own time both the engineers and accountants have sought protection for practicing engineers and accountants through professionalization. The threat was very real. How could a practicing engineer maintain his concern for public safety when asked to approve substandard work by a contractor or be replaced. Once professionalized, the reply to such a threat is "I can't approve your work as it is and you can't find another qualified engineer who will approve it." Just as the unions originally protected workers from management so the professions protect their members from external threat.

What is being protected is, of course, more than the individual practitioner. It includes the conditions, knowledge and skills which constitute that particular professional practice and in terms of which they perform their services. In traditional terms every adequate professional code will center around both the good it performs and the virtues required to perform it. The first is a straight consequential concern more easily stated than the second which is a reflective matter and usually takes some time to orchestrate. And both dimensions should be subject to alteration as conditions both inside and outside the profession warrant it. Management is not yet a profession. Perhaps, it never will be, but the need to reflect upon both dimensions, the virtues and the goods, of managerial practice is obvious for your own integrity as well as the integrity of the company for which you manage. Any extended treatment of what is involved is impossible here but something can be indicated in the following two examples.

In the discussion to follow it must be remembered that in each case there is a particular goal being given to practice and that the particular virtues dependent upon that goal are all hypothetically imperative. But also in each case the categorical conditions pertaining to practice in general apply and constitute the moral dimension.

The first such comes from the Preamble of the Code of Professional Responsibility of the Legal Profession. Let me quote and comment as needed. The Preamble begins:

> The continued existence of a free and democratic society depends upon recognition of the concept that justice is based upon the rule of law grounded in respect for the dignity of the individual and his capacity through reason for enlightened self-government. Law so grounded makes justice possible, for only through such law does the dignity of the individual attain respect and protection. Without it, individual rights become subject to unrestrained power, respect for law is destroyed, and rational self-government is impossible.[8]

The free, responsible society is the backdrop for this profession. Its chief function, its good, is to support and maintain the conditions of self-government as "guardians of the law." In the last paragraph of the Preamble we find concern for the virtue or excellence of function required by the individual member.

> Each lawyer must find within his own conscience the touchstone against which to test the extent to which his actions should rise above minimum standards. But in the last analysis it is the desire for the respect and confidence of the members of his profession and of the society which he serves that should provide to a lawyer the incentive for the highest possible degree of ethical conduct. The possible loss of respect and confidence is the ultimate sanction.[9]

The practice of lawyering is bi-polar, as are all other practices, and involves a particular service to a client. Both the good to the client and the virtue in service are determined by the framework of lawyering and are hypothetical in their imperativeness in that no one has to practice law. But both dimensions fall under the categorical concern for the ethical conditions of practice. There is one other idea in this Preamble that should be noted. Speaking of the variety of roles and tasks facing the practicing lawyer, it reads:

> Not every situation which he may encounter can be foreseen, but fundamental ethical principles are always present to guide him. Within the framework of these principles, a lawyer must with courage and foresight be able and ready to shape the body of the law to the ever-changing relationships of society.[10]

The interesting idea here is that in keeping with a free and responsible society of which lawyering is a part, this professional code is open-ended, leaving room for and encouraging individual responsibility in adapting to changing conditions.

The second example is a corporate statement:

The Beliefs of Borg-Warner: To Reach Beyond the Minimal

> Any business is a member of a social system, entitled to the rights and bound by the responsibilities of that membership. Its freedom to pursue economic goals is constrained by law and channeled by the forces of a free market. But these demands are minimal, requiring only that a business provide wanted goods and services, compete fairly, and cause no obvious harm. For some companies, that is enough. It is not enough for Borg-Warner. We impose upon ourselves an obligation to reach beyond the minimal. We do so convinced that by making a larger contribution to the society that sustains us, we best assure not only its future vitality, but our own. This is what we believe:
>
> **We believe in the dignity of the individual**
>
> However large and complex a business may be, its work is still done by people dealing with people. Each person involved is a unique human being, with pride, needs, values, and innate personal worth. For Borg-Warner to succeed, we must operate in a climate of openness and trust, in which each of us freely grants others the same respect, cooperation, and decency we seek for ourselves.
>
> **We believe in our responsibility to the common good**
>
> Because Borg-Warner is both an economic and social force, our responsibilities to the public are large. The spur of competition and the sanctions of the law give strong guidance to our behavior, but alone do not inspire our best. For that we must heed the voice of our natural concern for others. Our challenge is to supply goods and services that are of superior value to those who use them; to create jobs that provide meaning for those who do them; to honor and enhance human life; and to offer our talents and our wealth to help improve the world we share.
>
> **We believe in the endless quest for excellence**
>
> Though we may be better today than we were yesterday, we are not as good as we must become. Borg-Warner chooses to be a leader in serving our customers, advancing our technologies, and rewarding all who invest in us their time, money, and trust. None of us can settle for doing less than our best, and we can never stop trying to surpass what already has been achieved.
>
> **We believe in continuous renewal**
>
> A corporation endures and prospers only by moving forward. The past has given us the present to build on. But to follow our visions to the future, we must see the

difference between traditions that give us continuity and strength, and conventions that no longer serve us—and have the courage to act on that knowledge. Most can adapt after change has occurred; we must be among the few who anticipate change, shape it to our purpose, and act as its agents.

We believe in the commonwealth of Borg-Warner and its people

Borg-Warner is both a federation of businesses and a community of people. Our goal is to preserve the freedom each of us needs to find personal satisfaction while building the strength that comes from unity. True unity is more than a melding of self-interests; it results when values and ideals also are shared. Some of ours are spelled out in these statements of belief. Others include faith in our political, economic, and spiritual heritage; pride in our work and our company; the knowledge that loyalty must flow in many directions, and a conviction that power is strongest when shared. We look to the unifying force of these beliefs as a source of energy to brighten the future of our company and all who depend upon it.[11]

In the very first paragraph, the twin constraints of law and market forces are recognized as minimal demands upon a business. The company intends to go beyond these two and in doing so assure both the "future vitality" of their society and their own company. And to go beyond the minimum they assert their intention of instituting and encouraging the conditions that enable the margin of excellence in the practice of their employees. The language of the whole statement is moral in cast and its aim is excellence in business practice. Such excellence is inspired by "our natural concern for others." If it is asked upon what this "natural concern" is based, it might refer to the quite natural feelings most of us have for others. In this work, however, whatever feelings may or may not be present, we intend a concern based upon an adequate self-interest that can be understood reflectively and specified in terms of the enabling conditions of practice.

In the last half of Chapter Three we began by giving several examples of how the enabling conditions of the maintenance dimension are involved in individual practice of various sorts; classroom, familial and conversational practice. A central point was made; that self-interest, as a kind of practice, presupposes these enabling conditions. This is central because it means that all practice including that of business comes under the normative reach of these conditions. No matter what the goal may be, we have a vested interest in maintaining these conditions. Then, the Friedman view of the social responsibility of business was criticized for taking no account of the enabling conditions of practice, a reinterpretation was given of Adam Smith's Invisible Hand doctrine in terms of an adequate self-interest based upon the enabling conditions and this was extended in application to Kant's and Madison's Rationalism. Some current criticisms of managerial practice were brought up as context for application of these conditions and a comparison made between our economic and political systems with regard to them by way of preparing for further discussion in the context of the free market. It was also pointed out that the normative function of these enabling conditions is analogous to the prescriptive function of concepts.

In Chapter Four, the application of the enabling conditions to the study of individualism in the broader framework of American society as embodied in *Habits of the Heart*, *Individualism and Public Life* and *Ethics and Profits* was made.

Finally, in this Chapter Five, application of these enabling conditions was suggested as a basis for rights theory and contract theory, and an adequate understanding of the free market and of regulatory practice was shown to presuppose them. The importance of these applications lies in the fact that these enabling conditions have normative significance in practice and we turn to making that significance clear in the chapters to follow.

Footnotes

1. New York: Harcourt, Brace & World, Inc., 1920, p.24.

2. cf., #4, p. 14.

3. *The Individual and the Political Order*, Englewood Cliffs, NJ: Prentice-Hall, Inc., 1977, p. 78.

4. E&P, p. 51ff.

5. Englewood, NJ: Prentice-Hall, Inc., 1988, p. 181-2.

6. Ibid.

7. New York, NY: Warner Books, Inc., 1985, p. 5.

8. Chicago: American Bar Assoc., 1980, p.1.

9. Ibid.

10. Ibid.

11. Chicago, Il.: Borg-Warner Corporation, 1982.

The Imperatives of Practice and How They Arise

CHAPTER 6

In what has gone before, the two dimensions of practice were discussed as if they were separate parts of practice. I proceeded in that fashion because of the importance of the teleological or end-directed dimension for practice and because the major short-coming of that dimension—the grounding of moral obligation—would lead to consideration of the control or duty dimension. But it would be a mistake to take the Acquisitive and the Maintenance as two separate dimensions of practice centering around the goal and control poles respectively.

If you conceive of the Acquisitive as separate,—for example, the concern of egoism for the welfare of the self and the concern of Utilitarianism for the greatest number of selves, both of which are creatures of the means-end consequentialism of the Acquisitive, and both of which are deficient as explanations of the moral by themselves because they take no account of the enabling conditions of their own possibility under the threat which freedom of choice poses to them—, then from the Acquisitive as separate, no sense of moral obligation is forthcoming. Likewise, conceived separately, the Maintenance dimension constitutes a formalism and this is, I believe, one of the main reasons why Kant's categorical imperative is seen by many to be empty. From the perspective taken here, this is the consequence of divorcing the enabling conditions from what they enable and treating them as if they were self-standing. Hence, the emphasis upon the primacy of practice herein.

In this chapter the concern will be with how norms arise in practice, with the hypothetical and categorical norms arising in the two dimensions and with the relationship between these two dimensions or levels of practice traditionally called the prudential and the moral. In discussing the norms or constraints arising in these dimensions it will be pointed out and illustrated that the norm of prudence, usually located in the Acquisitive, means-end dimension, extends its reach beyond that dimension and that the moral norms, usually directed to the inner conditions of the Self in the Maintenance dimension, also extend beyond to the outer conditions of practice, to the World. These considerations will take us directly into the later Chapter on Justice and the Scope of the Moral. But let us begin by saying something about the critical and reflective aspect of consciousness as basic to our awareness of norms and limits and our ability to guide practice.

If it were not for the reflective or self-referential character of our consciousness which allows us to know that we know—to be aware we are aware—, we would be embedded in the content of consciousness, have no notion of limitation at all and be unable to carry on the guidance and control functions necessary to practice. Without this feature the comparative character basic to reasoning would be absent and there would be no foundation for judgment; for example, I feel pain, the pain is an object for me. An aspect of the self, expressed by the "I" in "I feel pain," extends beyond the pain. I am not the pain, although severe pain can sometimes blot out everything but itself, and this extending-beyond aspect is not separate but is dependent upon the content such that should the content be extinguished consciousness as such vanishes. It is, however, possible to lose yourself in what you are doing, for this extending-beyond aspect to be absorbed in content. But ordinarily, from this extending-beyond aspect I can compare this present pain with other remembered or expected states and can conclude, perhaps, that "this could be worse." We come to see the limits of a state or condition only in the midst of that state or condition. Practice involves this sort of thing in a very obvious way: being in one place and wanting to get to another, I ask what ought to be done to get there and the conditions which will enable me to get there are the norms which govern my getting there in practice. We recognize this as the means-end relation of the goal-oriented dimension of practice. But how do we go about practicing this means-end relation? If we must take Route 15 to get to Rochester, for instance, "taking Route 15" boils down in practice to staying within the limits marking out that route or, as the saying goes, "Keep between the fences." The fences are the limiting features in terms of which driving the car on Route 15 towards Rochester is accomplished. The theoretical and descriptive character of the means-as-conceived turns into the practical and prescriptive character of the means-to-be-employed in terms of the limiting conditions of that practice and they constitute operational norms for that practice. That is exactly how the yellow lines in the middle and on the sides of the road function at night under oncoming lights or in a dense fog. These will be recognized immediately as norms dependent upon the particular end chosen, universal only with regard to that particular end and limiting only in relation to that end. The limitations arising from the end chosen constitute the norms of the Acquisitive dimension and traditionally come under the values of "utility" or "prudence." The limitations arising from practice itself, no matter what end is chosen, constitute the norms of the Maintenance dimension and come traditionally under the "moral." Within practice, then, two levels of constraint arise and our question becomes what is the relation between the moral and the prudential dimensions.

Just as a limit is not wholly external to what it limits so, the moral level is not wholly external to the prudential level. A prudent act, that is, one effectively relating means to end does not occur in a vacuum. The moral conditions must be maintained while you are being prudent or else responsible practice becomes impossible. These moral constraints are satisfied when the prudent action is consistent with its own possibility. As such, maintaining the enabling conditions of practice is not just another consequence to be acquired in all practice. You can talk about them as ends if you wish and even aim at fostering them in your own practice. But they are to be *sustained while* acquiring the ends of your practice.

As long as goal-directed prudential activity falls within this set of boundary conditions there are no moral problems; actions are consistent with their own possibility and ends can be pursued in terms of their appropriate norms. Moral problems arise when the norms of a prudential goal or the goal itself fall outside of these boundary conditions and are in conflict with the norms of practice. The result is what was previously called a pragmatic contradiction. Such moral problems, though universal in scope are, none the less, personal in focus. In order to appreciate the way the Maintenance dimension limits—a better word, perhaps, would be surrounds—the Acquisitive, a comparison of two views and the development of a suggestion, all put forward by Kant, will be of help.

In the *Foundations*, an earlier work, the prudential and the moral are antithetical. Only when you act from duty are you moral. This position makes it impossible to be immoral. You are either moral or prudential and there is no room for the immoral within the moral where it belongs.

On the other hand, in *Religion Within the Limits of Reason Alone*, a later work, in recognition that, without the pull of the prudential and the sensuous, the moral would lose its authority, Kant holds that the moral condition is achieved by subordinating the prudential to the moral.[1] But this is not satisfactory either because it places the individual under a load of responsibility and guilt that not even a God can mediate and it tends to blunt completely the force of the prudential leaving no room for real reciprocity between the two. Kant suggests this reciprocity, himself, when, in speaking of the moral ought, he says:

> it is conceived... as an ought only in so far as he regards himself at the same time as a member of the world of sense[2]

Further, in the Third Critique, in discussing an organized product of nature, of which the Good Will is a primary example, he writes:

> A thing exists as a natural purpose if it is (although in a double sense) both cause and effect of itself.

and a little further on:

> An organized product of nature is one in which every part is reciprocally purpose (end) and means.[3]

He recognizes that only in the presence of the sensuous does the moral become a duty, and that only in the presence of the moral does the sensuous become a temptation. The notion of subordination is only partially expressive of this reciprocity. The view of this relationship presented here, in terms of a set of limiting conditions, the moral, and that which the set limits, the prudential, would appear to be more satisfactory since it marks out not only the moral as practice within this set of limits but the immoral as practice falling outside or undercutting them and the prudential as the goal-oriented aspect of practice in either case. The prudential is seen to fall within, and not under, the limits of the moral and is recognized as being constitutive of there being anything moral that ought to be done. Since I am here concerned with establishing the possibility of founding the moral in business practice, let us consider a hole-in-wall news-stand on the main street of a small city run by a single individual as a vehicle for spelling out how the normative arises in practice. The choice of this news-stand situation as example reflects several concerns. Perhaps an example involving an employee in a business establishment would be nearer the average; more people work for others than for themselves. But the choice of an individual entrepreneur running his own business reflects the individualism basic to this whole work as well as the emphasis upon entrepreneurship in current business thinking. The difference between the individual as entrepreneur and as manager for a firm is a matter of degree in the last analysis and the establishment of the moral outlines of individual practice comes before considering those of corporate practice.

Once you have committed yourself to running a news-stand there are a host of very practical "oughts" which descend upon you that, considered at a minimum, are constitutive of your being recognized, or being able to speak of yourself, as running a news-stand; renting a shop on which you can afford the rent in an area of the city having enough traffic to promise an income sufficient to support the business and yourself. This is not as easily done now as it once was with the predominance of shopping centers and the removal of much business from downtown, but for the sake of example, let us suppose. Also, some arrangement with the suppliers of newspapers and magazines must be made, but once you are set up and in business, "oughts" of a more regulative nature become important. At the center of these is the treatment you accord not only the people who purchase your goods but the people you depend upon and those who depend upon you. No doubt, you must be profitable to continue, no doubt, you ought to establish regular customers and no doubt, you ought to provide the best service you are capable of; all of these are very interrelated in very obvious ways. Also, quite obviously, the integrity of your own practice is closely tied up with the integrity of your business. If you hire another person to help, then how you treat that employee as a person has much to do with the integrity of that person's practice in your business. The moral and the prudential can run side by side and as I often hear people say, good ethics is good business. But some people for one reason or another don't seem able to practice successfully and the reasons for this can run the gamut of personal and social ills. Taken together, however, the way you handle these conditions forms your conception of how to run your business. Everyone in business has some such ideas and in the business books and magazines a succession of authors with varying credentials advance their perspective on these matters expressing their peculiar insights, practices, successes and failures. There is a sense in which these are the technical constraints of running a business but, however conceived, they are expressive of and presuppose choice, concern and consistency, the enabling conditions of a practicing Self.

Along with this system of ideas and operational principles clustering around the entrepreneur there is another such system of constraints constituted by the world in which you are doing business. To practice well or ill involves a context, in this case the city, and the conditions that its laws and ordinances maintain. The working conditions that enable individual businesses to sustain themselves and provide services for the city are of vital importance to your business. Also, the market conditions in the news and related industries place continually changing constraints upon your practice. There certainly are conditions without which no individual business could maintain itself and the citizens of the city, in need of such services, ought to see that such conditions exist to enable everyone to practice responsibly. Such systems of conditions presuppose multiplicity, continuity and structure, the enabling conditions of a World in which to practice. Because of freedom of choice these boundary or limiting conditions are in possible jeopardy at every turn of practice. Another and even more obvious object of concern is the ever-changing aspect of the competitive world of business, inherent risk in those conditions and the need to suit ones responses to those changes. There is a moral cast of care, consideration and respect that is as much a part of running your business as is competing as well as you can and better than your opponents, if possible. Properly running a business calls forth, exercises and sustains all of these dimensions, including an inseparable sense of the moral, not by importing anything foreign from the outside but by being aware in practice of the rights and duties, the freedoms and disciplines, resident in business practice itself. Many of these have been put into laws and regulations but in the last analysis, while such external constraints may point to, suggest and punish failure to comply, continuing successful practice is a matter of self-discipline in response to both the inner and outer conditions of your business.

In the foregoing example, I have wanted to emphasize the interrelatedness of the norms functioning in that activity. Using the Kantian three types of imperatives, the technical, concerned with the skills used in the business, the prudential, concerned with the successful carrying on of the business and the moral, concerned with maintaining the possibility of activity itself, three levels could have been marked out. But then they would have been separated and above all I wanted to show that in practice they do not occur as separate; the technical involves and shades into the prudential and together they are the occasion of the moral. Now having pointed out the indigeneity of these norms to practice, it is time to delimit the moral and its relation to the prudential more carefully.

Previously, we said that an act is "right" if consistent with its own possibility. Also, that most questions of right and wrong fall under the Maintenance dimension and can be handled in terms of the enabling conditions of practice. But practice is complex in nature and there are moral considerations beyond the norms of maintenance so far pointed out. In order to convey this complexity as best I can, in what follows, we shall consider first the Acquisitive dimension as the arena for imperatives of the hypothetical sort derived from particular ends chosen. It is under this hypothetical sort that questions of utility and prudence have come to be considered and it is here that the reach of prudence beyond the hypothetical will be considered. Secondly, the Maintenance dimension will be considered as the arena for the protection of the enabling conditions conceived as rights and as imperatives of the categorical sort. Finally, in a later chapter we shall consider the relationship of these two dimensions of practice to each other in terms of the idea of "just practice."

a) Hypothetical Imperatives

One of the distinguishing features of practice, you will recall, is that through it some state, capacity, condition or thing not now present to the practicing agent is made present or actual. Practice reaches beyond itself and in terms of this transcending function we are able to grow, develop and sustain ourselves as well as build and make things. In so doing the self is directly involved with something other than itself, the means are connected to the end, the control pole to the goal pole, the inner self to the outer world. In practice, the radical separation of the so-called subject-object split is overcome.

An imperative is a command, a directive to do or refrain from doing something. An hypothetical imperative tells us something is to be done because it will tend to produce a certain result. Thus the command is conditional upon our wanting that result. Example: if you want to be healthy, then you ought to eat properly. All the "oughts" of the Acquisitive dimension are of this hypothetical kind. You can get out from under the "ought" required by any particular goal by denying that you want that goal. Every goal of practice has imperatives appropriate to it and acceptance of the goal places you under the appropriate imperatives. If you want to learn to hit a long iron out of a sand trap, given a decent lie, there are certain things you must do and by reflection upon what you want and how to achieve it with the materials at hand, you arrive at a set of variations on your golf swing imperative for accomplishing that purpose. The necessity, of course, is hypothetical. You can use a "hand mashie" instead and go on about your business. But not if you are committed to *playing golf*. In this particular example there are a number of things to do, but perhaps the overriding imperative is to have the club-face hit the ball before it hits the sand. Notice that you must be acquainted with the activity in question before there is anything to reflect upon and before talk about and conceptualization of the practice will be meaningful. Direct acquaintance is undoubtedly most useful but some kinds of practice are closely related to others and similarities foster understanding through analogy. And, of course, all practice shares the generic features we have been discussing. Another example will bring out the hypothetical and even the tentative character of different kinds of practice.

Suppose you intend to walk a straight line from A to B. In order to do so, on the one hand, you must put one foot in front of the other and, on the other hand, you must keep your balance. In this example not only is there an interchange of means and ends, one becoming the other, as Dewey pointed out in his famous article, but these two poles of practice function both descriptively and normatively in reciprocal relation to one another. Keeping ones balance is a means to forward motion toward B and yet it is also an end in itself, a condition of my being able to move myself at all. If I begin to lose my balance, I can cease forward movement until I feel it regained or, perhaps, if I am close to B and in a race, I can move more quickly and reach B before falling down. The example illustrates the complexity and multi-dimensionality of practice. Speaking from the external goal-pole, what is aimed at must be attained and speaking from the internal control-pole, the conditions of self-government must be maintained. In trying to steal second base, the runner undoubtedly increases his chances of success, if the catcher's throw is close, by sliding, but in sliding he cuts down on his chances to take third should the defense bungle the play. It is common knowledge in pool and billiards that consideration of the desirable position for the next shot should be included in the plans for making the shot in front of you. Of course, if you miss the shot in front of you, you have lost your balance and are flat on your back.

As previously stated, since at least the time of Kant the concern for consequences has been understood as falling under the norms of prudence and as completely separated from moral and ethical norms. In our language, the Acquisitive dimension is the arena of prudential and hypothetical norms dependent upon the end aimed at and the Maintenance dimension the arena of moral and categorical norms to which we shall turn later on. But in an ethic of practice it is not possible to separate the two so completely. Speaking in the context of practice, the imperative "Be prudent" in the concern for consequences is as important morally as any other. After all, it is the purposive character of practice that is constitutive of the whole moral domain; without some end or purpose there would be nothing that I ought to do in any sense of an imperative. As such it must not be excluded from moral consideration on pain of leaving the moral ought empty and unsupported. Arguments have been advanced showing that Kant, himself, was not unaware that the general concern for consequences, no matter what the end, was categorical. Only a being that is reflective can be concerned with how it is doing what it is doing and we must look more closely at what the imperative "Be prudent!" means for practice.

First, we must consider the restrictive use of the term "prudence" alluded to before as peculiar to modern usage, especially in ethics. If we ask what "Be prudent!" means, it is a council much like "Be careful!" which concerns how you practice without saying anything about the end involved. But it goes further than just how you practice. There is also a sense of "in the face of," including the routine and expected and extending beyond to the new and the unexpected. But, beginning in the early modern period, the dominant strain in ethics has focused upon the self as an atomic particular with emphasis upon self-interest and self-advantage, and prudence has come to be associated with egoism, in fact, as its primary virtue, with self-interest as the obvious end of prudence and included in the meaning of the term itself. No doubt that is one of the ends to which prudence can be directed but it should be clear that prudence need not be restricted to that end. Nor should prudence be limited to particular means-ends relations in the Acquisitive dimension. In fact, dictionaries include the wider and older usage deriving from the Latin "prudentia"; for example,

> a) Wisdom shown in the exercise of reason, fore-thought and self-control; b) sagacity or shrewdness in the management of affairs (as of government or business) shown in the skillful selection, adaptation and use of means to a desired end; c) providence in the use of resources; d) attentiveness to possible hazard or disadvantage.[4]

In the wider sense, prudence means not only adequate care in handling affairs, but wisdom regarding possible future contingencies. In this wider sense prudence is very much a part of practical reason and a central feature of practice. In that prudence can be thought of as care and wisdom in the relating of means to ends, it would seem to belong in the acquisitive dimension with its concern for particular ends. But the imperative "Be prudent" appears also to belong to the Maintenance dimension as a directive for handling all ends whatever. Certainly, practice that did not take into account its own limiting and enabling conditions would not be judged to be prudent practice. Prudential concern for the norms required by any particular goal of practice give rise to the hypothetical concern for consequences in practice as well as the categorical concern for the enabling conditions of practice itself. The concern for all consequences undergirds the concern for any consequence. Prudence of the hypothetical, means-end sort is positive and reaches beyond to the goal. Prudence of the categorical sort, however, reaches beyond also but only in a negative way reflective of the meaning under d), above, in its definition, "attentiveness to possible hazard or disadvantage." The openness of experience subjects all practice to changing circumstances that may at the least require changes in practice and at most damage or remove the very possibility of practice. Prudence of this categorical sort extends the moral beyond mere maintenance and we shall return to it after the moral imperative of the Maintenance dimension has been considered in the next section.

b) The Categorical Imperative

When we attempt to come up with a general norm or imperative for the Maintenance dimension a very simple one suggests itself in the term "maintenance": certain capacities are to be protected and encouraged in the individual that are necessary for responsible practice. These capacities are given expression in our moral standards and imperatives and we phrase them both negatively and positively. In positive terms, "Be truthful!" gives a direction to practice and the negative "Don't lie!" tells you to avoid lying as a means to whatever your end may be. It is interesting to note the relationship between the positive and negative forms of these imperatives. The negative "Don't lie!," for example, which I take to be categorical, sets forth one of the limitations upon practice, but it can be objectified in a positive "Be truthful!" as an end for practice and thus rendered hypothetical. If you take this positive form as basic then the justification for why you ought to be truthful must be in terms of the goods consequent upon being truthful. In this positive form you have an ethic of virtue where virtue is considered as excellence of function, and any given virtue is determined, to use the best known example in our tradition, as the mean between two extremes.[5] : courage is the mean between cowardice and foolhardiness, where the virtue and its two vices are ranged along a continuum of ends related in terms of excess and deficiency. But the positive form is always open to the question "Why should I be virtuous?" and depends for the force of its obligation upon the acceptance of a desired consequence. Here, the moral is strictly in the realm of the consequential, our Acquisitive dimension. On the other hand, however, in the negative form, what was a virtue becomes a limit within which your choice in practice must fall to be consistent with its own possibility. In an ethic of practice the enabling conditions are ranged around end-directed practice as a horseshoe of limiting conditions upon self-governing practice. Such an ethic sets out your duty in confronting the temptation of ends and the pressure of needs, and failure to respect these limits is self-stultifying and a pragmatic contradiction. Any such council of restraint can be turned into an end to be attained; any categorical imperative can be turned into one that is hypothetical. From a theoretical point of view such objectification is always possible and very useful for analysis and understanding. But such transformation renders moral obligation nugatory. One of the virtues of holding practice to be basic is that it prevents such transformation from being the last word in ethics. All imperatives cannot be hypothetical.

If our analysis of practice as bi-polar is correct then it is impossible to reduce or explain away one pole in terms of the other as much of contemporary ethics seems to do in either deontological or consequential theories. The latter, by itself, cannot generate any sense of responsibility for its own principles and the former, by itself, tends to be empty. An ethic of practice has to live with this and its implications are significant, I believe, for ethics in general. The most important consequence is that ethics cannot be a seamless robe covering all dimensions of human practice with some single, generalized rule. This is so because practice, the occasion and locus of that degree of freedom and of responsibility persons are able to exercise for themselves, is *jointed* and, as exemplified in the pragmatic contradiction, can be at odds with itself. And, of course, when any practice is at odds with itself it is at odds with the practice of any self.

In connection with this point and of help in laying out the topography of the Maintenance dimension, consideration of the relationship between the justly celebrated forms of Kant's categorical imperative will be useful.

Students of Kant are often puzzled by the different formulations of the categorical imperative in that Kant considered this imperative to be one and the supreme moral principle and yet he gives several formulations of it which appear to say different things. It has been pointed out in criticism that the first formulation—"act only according to that maxim by which you can at the same time will that it become a universal law"[6]—conflicts with the third formulation—"act so that you treat humanity, whether in your own person or that of another, always as an end and never as a means only."[7] For instance, to aid a lawbreaker is clearly wrong because if it were universalized, the conditions for such an act would be destroyed. On the other hand, if the lawbreaker is turned in, he is being treated as a means to the maintenance of the law rather than as an end-in-himself. There appears to be a legitimate criticism here. But I think it is based on a misunderstanding, one which Kant himself helps to foster when he gives the impression that the categorical imperative is the test for the acceptability of a proposed act. Of course, when he does this he blurs his own insight, for, in spite of the fact that he says it is,[8] the categorical imperative is not a criterion for specific acts. No doubt it can be used as such but the difficulty pointed out above arises unless it is also understood that the categorical imperative is intended to reveal those character traits (the anatomy of a Good Will, Kant's ultimate value,) which are consistent with themselves and non-destructive of themselves when they characterize the quality of an agent's willing: it is right to tell a lie only if it is right (possible) to be a liar. When this is kept in mind, it will be readily apparent that the act that maintains one's own integrity as a rational will, also maintains the same integrity for all wills. (Here we come upon a root meaning of the term "liberal"— a liberal attitude not only preserves my own integrity but the acts continuous with it preserve the integrity of all who come in contact with it. In the light of this classical meaning of the term, our contemporary usage of "liberal," indicating centralized governmental control, can be seen as a perversion and antithetical to individualism.)

In his explanation of the first formulation stated above, Kant gives examples of acts whose principles do not qualify as universal law and morally right because one, suicide, "would contradict itself"[9] and the other, not keeping promises, "could never count as a universal law of nature and still agree with itself"[10] Based on these considerations the categorical imperative is often stated as "act so that the maxim of your action can be universalized without contradiction." But it should be pointed out that the self-contradiction involved in his famous four examples[11] does not appear to be logical contradiction but rather what we have called pragmatic contradiction, instead. Kant himself calls them "contradictions in our own volition"[12] and not contradictions in content.

Viewed from the perspective of an ethic of practice, the various formulations of the categorical imperative appear to be different and even in conflict because they each express differing aspects of the context of practice itself for which they are categorical. In this light, the first formulation is expressive of humans as acting agents, while the third formulation is expressive of humans as ends-in-themselves. Kant himself says "that action which is consistent with the autonomy of the will is permitted"[13] and this yields another formulation which mediates between the other two—"act only on that maxim which will enable you to maintain continuous autonomy in willing." Taken together these three—as initiating agent, as end-in-itself and as autonomous willing— express the organic dynamism Kant calls the Good will.

In what I have been saying, another version of the categorical imperative—an act should be consistent with its own possibility—has been used rather than any one of the three versions pointed out in Kant. Actually, from the moral point of view Kant's third formulation—treating people as ends and not merely as means only—cannot be improved upon and is itself an improvement on the Golden Rule. But "being consistent with its own possibility" has been emphasized here because I want to point up, 1) the self-referential character of this imperative and, 2) the fact that it concerns not only all of everyone else's acts but all of mine as well—Universalization without self-contradiction is most often explained by "it would be right for everyone." I referred to this as the common sense meaning of "right" previously, (p. 26). This puts the emphasis upon universalizability as essential to the moral, but the emphasis should be placed on consistent application in practice by anyone or everyone. "Consistent with its own possiblity" does this. Finally, this rendition indicates, as nearly as I know how to, that its imperativeness is fundamentally a logical matter—the logic of reflective practice—and not in any sense merely a principle favoring long-run consequences.

Earlier, in considering prudence, I claimed that "Be prudent" was categorically imperative, also; be prudent in putting means to ends whatever those means and ends may be in any case. "Being honest" is consistent with its own possibility. "Being dishonest" is not. Is "Being prudent" consistent in the same way? I believe it is, but, over and above putting means to ends, prudence means taking everything into account that can reasonably be considered as affecting your practice. This covers the enabling conditions, as was said previously, but it also extends to include the structures or forces in the outer world whose impact upon your practice will make a difference. It is not my intent to raise "Be prudent" to the heights as the most general formulation of the categorical imperative. It is a directive for the conducting of all and every practice and not an enabling condition of practice. Ones concern for it in practice is categorical and to make clear why, something must be said about the categorical itself.

The "categorical" is the unconditioned, the independent, as opposed to the conditioned and dependent. It is the opposite of the "hypothetical" which is dependent, as explained previously. There is not much to be said in modern logic for the categorical proposition such as "All men are mortal." For what I take to be good and sufficient reasons, not to the point here, modern logic treats propositions of that type as meaning "For every x, if x is a man, then x is mortal" which conditions x's mortality upon x's being a man and this is a hypothetical, conditional, if-then, statement. Scientific explanation is the best example of this conditional understanding. Kant, who applied "categorical" to ethical imperatives, wrote before this modern distinction in logic was made. But, considering the importance for his theory of the difference between categorical and hypothetical imperatives, if the categorical is translated into hypothetical terms, a radical alteration has occurred, not of a logical but a substantive kind. Many contemporary thinkers would deny the possibility of the categorical on these grounds. If Kant were allowed to speak, he would undoubtedly say, among other things, that morality presupposes humans are free to do what they ought to do and such a free act would be unconditioned, one not determined by antecedent conditions. The imperative or law for such a free and moral act would be unconditioned also and categorical. So the use of the term "categorical" is directly tied to one of the most important characteristics of human practice, locus of free choice. If you take freedom seriously as Kant does and if you take freedom as lawful action as Kant does and not simply the absence of law, then the law of free persons will be categorical. Thus, are the universal principles of the law and the particular actions of the individual brought together in the reflective capacities for practice of individuals in the ethical theory of this greatest of modern thinkers.

But the sense in which "Be prudent" extends beyond the enabling conditions of the control pole and encompasses not only the shape of our purposiveness but our concern with the contingencies of the world of experience is an important part of the jointedness of practice mentioned earlier. It will be treated more fully hereafter but the sense in which the maintenance dimension expresses categorical concern for the outer as well as the inner world is an essential aspect of the moral imperatives of practice.

I have wanted to set forth an ethic centered on the same kind of organic dynamism as found in practice rather than in the Good Will because, apart from the context of practice, the Good Will is, by itself, empty. Or put in another way, it is important that the Good Will be Good not only for itself and for all other Wills but that its Goodness arises in the context of responsible practice where moral obligation has its roots.

So far then, practice is basic for humans. Outside of the context of practice humans are not morally responsible and only in that context does moral responsibility arise. But practice has two dimensions, one, the purposive, means-ends orientation of the acquisitive dimension, the other, the two sets of enabling conditions without which practice could not be. The imperatives generated by the former are hypothetical and derived from the particular end involved. The enabling conditions of practice itself are categorically imperative in the context of practice. They are the conditions of individual freedom, responsible practice and of being a person. Under the press of need, the desire for ends and the use of choice those conditions can be undercut and destroyed. It is to be remembered that our needs and desires may differ but these enabling conditions are the same for everyone. It would be easy to set up a morality for the maintenance of these enabling conditions, and, as Kant says in his later work, subordinate happiness to virtue or, for us, the Acquisitive to the Maintenance dimension. This is certainly an important moral consideration because what you may lose in wrong practice is what makes you or anyone else able to acquire anything at all. And so it is undoubtedly true that the pursuit of consequences must be carried on within the limitations of everyone's capacities for practice; as Kant held, happiness is good but only if you are virtuous. And many, perhaps most, of the situations calling for moral judgments can be handled this way in terms of the categorical imperative as we have formulated it. But the jointedness of practice spoken of previously seems to indicate that the moral extends beyond merely the subordination of the Acquisitive to the Maintenance dimension. In what way the moral is to be extended is I believe hinted at in Kant's later work when he says that prudential concern is constitutive of the moral ought and that only in the light of the moral ought does prudential concern in any particular case become a temptation. As we said before, subordination is not an adequate rendition of the reciprocal relation between Kant's moral and prudential or our own Acquisitive and Maintenance dimensions. We must explore this matter in search of a more adequate rendition. And I want to start this exploration in the next chapter by considering the ancient, very honorable and, in many ways, supreme virtue, justice.

Footnotes

1. Greene, T.M.,& Hudson, H.H., trs., New York: Harpur & Brothers, 1960, pp. 25, 31.
2. FMM, p. 74.
3. *Critique of Judgment*, Bernard, J.H., tr., New York: Hafner Publishing Co.,1951, pp, 132-3.
4. *Webster Third New International Dictionary*, 1961.
5. cf. Aristotle's *Nichomachean Ethics.*
6. FMM, p. 39.
7. FMM, p. 47.
8. FMM, pp. 31, 40.
9. FMM, p. 39.
10. FMM, p. 40.
11. FMM, pp. 39-41.
12. FMM, p. 42.
13. FMM, p. 58.

Justice and the Scope of the Moral

CHAPTER 7

In the previous chapter, in marking out the character of the imperatives stemming from the two dimensions of practice, it was pointed out, in a provisional way, that these two dimensions cannot be conceived as mutually exclusive. It is true that the hypothetical imperative is centered around the particular end in view in practice and the categorical imperative centers on the enabling conditions of practice. It is also true that in large part moral action is a matter of the subordination of the Acquisitive to the Maintenance dimension, of the subordination of the utility of consequences to the preservation of the conditions of practice, a concern for rights. But in treating the idea of "prudence" as an imperative it was suggested that, while what is prudent for any particular case depends upon the particular end in view, there is something categorical about the imperative "Be prudent!" And yet you cannot say that prudence is an enabling condition of practice in the same sense as choice, concern and consistency are. You can limit prudence to suiting means to ends but as we pointed out its meaning is much broader than that and can be understood to have reference to both dimensions without falsification. Further, it was suggested that this reaching beyond the inner conditions of action which the categorical evidences, for example, in prudence, may be brought about by the jointedness of practice. If this is so then you are not going to be able to place all of man's moral concerns under one blanket, under one general principle. What this would mean for an ethic of practice needs investigating and we shall begin to do so in considering the nature of justice.

Most often these days we hear about justice as a social virtue, a just law or social action as applied to a human community of some sort. And it most often concerns how the benefits or burdens of individual or community action fall upon the members of that community. Under the idea of justice these benefits and burdens are judged from two different perspectives, equal treatment for all concerned and treating each as each deserves or treating each fairly. The symbol for justice is the lovely lady, wearing a blindfold, with a balance in her hand and it is generally agreed that the completely just balance of equality and desert is not apt to be encountered in this world. We must, however, do the best we can, for, where justice is concerned, matters of degree are of first importance. These two concerns of justice, equality and desert, arise from the two-dimensional character of practice itself; the means-ends concern for consequences and ends, on the one hand, and the concern for the enabling conditions as capacities in the individual to be fostered and maintained, on the other. Both of these dimensions are embodied in the formal principle of distributive justice which holds that equals should be treated equally and unequals unequally in proportion to their relevant differences. For example, a bequest which treated all employees equally without concern for length of personal commitment in the service rendered would be considered lacking in justice, as being unfair. Or, giving the testimony of a known liar equal weight in court with that of average witnesses would not be just. Not only is justice concerned with the rights of individuals comparatively but also with how those protected capacities have been exercised by persons in the matter at hand, individual desert. How one has practiced often qualifies ones rights, one way or another, with regard to the just distribution of benefits and burdens. The wonderful song of the Mikado, "Let the Punishment Fit the Crime," sets forth the same ideal of harmonic suitability in matters of punishment (retributive justice) between deed and doer as is expressed in the distributive principle between benefit or burden and recipient.

Looked at in this way, the ancient principle of justice goes much more deeply into the moral groundwork than merely as a social consequence. In Plato's *Republic* for example, the talk is of what constitutes a just soul. It is said that justice in the soul is found when every capacity or power of the soul has its appropriate virtue or measure; Reason has Truth, Spirit has Courage and Appetite, having no measure of its own, has Temperance imposed upon it by Reason. A just soul is the harmony under Reason of these three functions. For us, a just practice is one that is consistent with its own possibility in the way we have been discussing, one in which the two dimensions of practice are not out-of joint but compatible. When these two dimensions are consistent with each other, it is incorrect to say the acquisitive is subordinated to the maintenance. The joining of means to ends to fulfill or complete a purpose, the exercise of the capacities for choice, concern and consistency in the pursuit of some particular goal, place a set of limitations on that practice which, if over-stepped, render that practice inconsistent with itself. But it does not destroy that practice although it may significantly limit your capacity for practice in general. It will, however, rule out the choosing of certain means as well as certain ends because they are inconsistent with responsible practice. Because of the jointedness of practice and because the success of practice is subject to the power of contingent external events, it is not guaranteed that if you practice responsibly you will succeed; there is no necessary connection between virtue and happiness, as Kant would put it. But certainly you have a better chance and are far more able to succeed if your practice is responsible. The hope for a new manager is that he will manage "well." Undoubtedly, "managing well" encompasses the possibility of success, but whether success is possible or not, "managing well" includes managing responsibly. It has reference to both dimensions of practice in the same way justice includes both, only the former refers to results in both while the latter concerns the relation between the two. But now we must reintroduce the problem with prudence that was put aside earlier.

Prudence, in the narrow, modern sense spoken of before, (p. 73ff), has to do with reason as an instrument for suiting means to ends chosen in the service of some need or desire. Prudence in this sense is very nearly equivalent to the scientific method applied in every day use within the acquisitive dimension. This is the sense of "science" used in economics and management science, so-called, among others. The broader usage of prudence which was adopted here refers to reason not merely as an instrument for successfully suiting means to ends not determined by reason but to reason as playing an important part in the determination of ends, also. This function of reason is exemplified in the criterion for right action we have advanced; "consistent with its own possibility" is the reflective use of reason central to practice that we have been discussing. Reason's part in determining ends for practice lies in the limiting conditions which constrain practice. In the analysis of practice, I have tried to show that practice has a dimension of the instrumental, means-ends use of reason but that it also has a dimension of the end-determining use of reason. Certainly in terms of this analysis of practice, adequate prudential concern would encompass the relation an action would have to the conditions of its own possibility, the self-referential aspect, as well as to the relation of an action to possible consequences and the risks to be incurred. This extended concern for the two dimensions means that in the last analysis the acquisitive dimension is of moral concern. I do not mean by this that the acquisitive, by itself, is of moral concern, but that the categorical concern of the maintenance dimension extends beyond the inner conditions and takes into account the push of purpose and the impact of events in the outside world.

It is true that a wrong choice will reduce, damage or destroy the ability to practice of any agent. But, as was brought out in talking about positive and negative rights, negative rights, to protect and maintain the capacities for choice, concern and consistency in peoples' practice, need some support; a person who is ill or starving or ignorant or afraid of what he does, cannot practice effectively and responsibly. If we want people to practice effectively and responsibly then some minimum set of positive conditions must be in place to keep those capacities for practice in a condition to be adequately exercised. But this is not to be understood as saying that conditions adversely effecting responsible practice should be remedied by the community. And here is where the aforementioned jointedness of practice brings about difficulties. We have a phrase, "Help others to help themselves" which combines the two joints justly—perhaps a system of public education, with all its attendant difficulties, comes closest to doing this—but the phrase is more easily uttered than implemented in areas other than education. Public support for education can be such a success because education takes time, requires practice by the individual receiving the external benefit and, most importantly, speaks directly to the capacities belonging to the maintenance dimension of practice and to the self-discipline required in their exercise and continuence. Jobs as a benefit can also speak directly to these capacities for responsible practice provided such opportunities constitute real practice and not just "make work." Many of the other types of benefits provide some end needed or desirable but only indirectly related to the capacities of the maintenance dimension. In emergency situations where temporary relief is required such benefits are wholly in keeping but as an ongoing condition they tend to blunt and dissipate these capacities for practice. When an economic system has more people than it has real opportunities for responsible practice it cannot help but begin to destroy its own enabling conditions and those of its people. Unless the internal conditions of practice are effectively engaged, any external benefit becomes a dole and cannot be said to have the basic needs and interests of its recipients in mind.

With respect to the maintenance of these inner conditions of choice, concern and consistency, it is never the case that only if such and such material conditions are present am I able to be moral and responsible. Somewhere in his writings C. I. Lewis says that this moral sense may be presumed in humans. The alternative is to be driven by whips or lured by bait. Just as the law does not recognize ignorance of the law as a condition, neither can a community recognize the absence of a moral sense based upon the reflective awareness of these enabling conditions. These capacities are natural to humans and must be presumed so, even though they require nurture and development for full expression. In the absence of such a presumption it could not be argued at all convincingly that we place the highest value on the individual.

Just practice, as we have described it, may be an ideal difficult of attainment but it constitutes a description of that presumption without which our individualism is empty. Moral responsibility does not arise out of or rest upon these enabling conditions. It comes with them and as previously indicated is both individual and social in its application. Some developmental stages, such as those put forth by Kohlberg and others, are involved prior to maturity. The traditional way of conceiving and ordering such stages as beginning in a narrow egoism and then progressing outward until at last, at moral maturity, the good of others is somehow factored in, seems to stem from that same modern assumption of the atomic individual which was noted before in the understanding of prudence. As Bishop Butler pointed out long since, humans have concerns and affections for many things other than themselves. Undoubtedly, they must balance these against their own survival and well-being but self does not precede the world. It is certainly true that they can become selfish and self- centered but just as certainly it is false that human nature is originally built that way and unable to take interest in anything other than itself. Even the "enlightened self-interest" advocated by the Research and Policy Committee of the Committee for Economic Development[1] which councils indirection in self-interest rather than the more direct and crude variety, is an inadequate substitute for the moral presumption about which we have been talking. Nor is this presumption of a moral sense merely a postulate grounded in hope or benevolence or altruism concerning the people with whom we deal. This presumption is grounded in the enabling conditions and is co-extensive with them. The poverty of ones world or the habituation to the instrumental use of reason may mitigate against the full recognition of the self-referential use of reason we have been advocating. As previously pointed out, these conditions operate in practice whether you are aware of them or not. In the last analysis even the crassest instance of self-interest shadows forth the conditions of its own possibility and renders this moral presumption a matter of degree and adequate recognition and not something that can be denied without pragmatic contradiction. Surely, this situation is the underpinning for our preference for talking rather than action between nation states; dialogue facilitates, stimulates and requires this self-referential dimension of reason to a greater extent than does overt action. It is not just that talk is preferable to violence, which it very often is, but that the conditions of dialogue already presuppose a degree, however small, of agreement and the possibility of its extension. This is not the peace-at-any-price view often associated with contemporary liberalism. The enabling conditions of practice place limits upon not only what you ought to do, but what you ought to suffer in such matters. Let us take the suggestions put forward so far about the nature of practice and construct a model that expresses their unity and relatedness. It will be an exercise in framing a conception under the constraints of both the moral and the prudential, the ideal and the real, and will spell out the context of practice in which the ideal of justice arises and to which it is applied. But, to begin with, let me put the whole matter in a setting of business practice.

Several years ago I was privileged to be a participant in a program on ethics and management the principal speaker of which was the new CEO of a large and well-known corporation. He had taken on the job of reorganizing that company to stave off possible Chapter 11 status. He recounted how, when first assuming control, his choices were necessitated by survival rather than considerations of moral right or wrong; all decisions were grey and it was only after some time and some progress in the rescue operation had been made that decisions instead of being bathed in survival grey gradually began wearing the morally black and white colors normally present in decision making. He then went on to wonder just what conditions must be present in order to allow such return to black and white normalcy, and which, if known, might indicate the approach of survival grey for a company. His wondering about these conditions presupposes that the moral is not something external to but an integral element of business practice.

The limiting conditions existing in a given corporate situation can not be marked off without reference to that particular situation but perhaps something can be said about practice which if not wholly satisfactory may be in the right direction.

It was said previously, that within any practice two levels of constraints arise, one having to do with the end aimed at and one with the enabling conditions of practice itself. It was also suggested that the enabling conditions of practice surround the acquisitive dimension of practice in horse-shoe fashion as a set of limitations upon both the means and ends chosen in that dimension. To employ a spatial metaphor, it is the room allowed by these limitations that makes the difference to practice. Choice requires alternatives, either other ends than the one chosen or other means than the ones chosen. In the case of the corporation referred to above, the CEO was brought in to preserve the viability of the company as a practicing concern. The decisions needed to carry out this purpose were all bathed in grey; there was no room for anything but choices of the narrowest financial kind, choices which under normal and happier conditions would not even recommend themselves. But, what is involved in "having no room?" It means, at least, that only one course of action would do the job, not little by little over a period of time, but as quickly as possible. There are several elements here which can bring that horse-shoe of limitations down so tightly around the practice of the corporation that survival necessitates certain moves, all of which are grey because of their necessity. No one blames an individual for defending himself when survival is threatened and a company can be in a very similar situation. That is not to suggest, however, that moral blame be withheld in the corporate instance for, in such survival operations, many people may be greatly harmed and, quite often, as the direct result of bad management to begin with. More to the point, time is denied, a response is required, now. Practice requires time because, except in such survival situations, it is a complex of goals, requirements and limitations that must be carried along, furthered or at least considered and accounted for. My friends in business are always talking about trade-offs. Since you can't have everything, you must balance things out to remain viable. But in the survival situation you don't have the luxury of trade-offs. Necessity rules! It is the shortest of short-run situations. Obviously, no business can run from day to day. Somewhere, Peter Drucker wrote that profits are how you pay for tomorrow. I take that to mean that we buy time to allow for management of, instead of only response to, our tomorrow. This is no argument for the long-run. Differing elements of corporate practice require differing time spans to keep the complex of interrelated means and ends in proper trim. There is no other security in life and that is as good a way to understand the meaning and function of civilization as I know of. The constraints of practice itself, the horse-shoe of limitations, must be kept close enough to practice, and yet, far enough removed from it, to permit the interplay of the multiplicity of corporate as well as human ends. Chapter 11 is just such a mechanism for extending time to preserve values through revised practice rather than succumbing to the destructive necessities of bankruptcy.

The above considerations take us a step or two further along in explaining the relation between the non-linear of the two levels of practice, with its continuous centering upon the conditions of practice and the linear level, with its reaching towards the particular goals of practice.

In order to look into the ways and reasons why moral concern extends beyond the maintenance dimension, we should look into why opinion has it that Lady Justice is never able to balance her scale completely. One very obvious reason is the blindfold she wears. But why should Justice be blind? And how does this lack of sight affect her moral judgments. The usual answer to this question, I think, has to do with the incommensurateness of the two requirements of equality and desert, individual desert seems to mitigate equality. Added to this, if the Lady be human, is an inability to know what any individual really deserves because she can only infer from behavior and cannot see into motives and capacities adequately. No doubt this is part of the cause of blindness but considering Justice in relation to the bi-polarity and jointedness of practice as we are, suggests other considerations as well that will shed light on our question.

Back in Chapter Five in suggesting that the ongoing development of a legal system reflects the bi-polar character of practice in that a right, freedom of speech, for example, is given ideal expression, as I just expressed it, around the self-pole of practice, and the needed limitations or constraints on that ideal, for example, clear and present danger, are given expression around the world-pole of practice as experience requires them. Theoretically, I have the right to free speech, but, practically, that right is understood and applications made through the essential limitations which experience has shown necessary and which mark out this element of the legal system from other elements. And this task is never complete because change is real and experience is the open door to tomorrow. These points suggest something similar as applying to our present question of Justice.

One further reason why the Lady is blind is because experience keeps modifying the limitations needed under differing circumstances and this modifies the meaning and application of our ideals or rights, or, in the case of Justice, the constraints upon equality and desert. And this means that in an ethic of practice what the just practice will be in any situation is a matter of individual judgment. The moral responsibility rests with the individual, and, while there is a whole civilization of ideals and their limitations, some long-standing and some current, some insightful and some wrong-headed, to act as guides in choosing, the responsibility for practice cannot be removed unless the status of the person is modified. If there were a right rule for everything we do, there would be no premium upon wise judgment, know-how and creativity, and no reason for valuing the individual so highly.

I am not denying that some rules are better than others nor that we can understand and appreciate the difference between the better and the worse. It seems we are always trying to put structure before people. It would be so simple if it could be done. We have just come through an extended period of emphasis upon methodology spurred, I expect, by the successes of the scientific method. A good teacher, so it went, could teach any subject, a good manager could manage any business. What is needed are the rules and operational principles of your discipline. Even ethics is treated in this operationally formal fashion very often. And I can understand that, when business or education is expanding and a quantity of the best possible managers and teachers are needed, that is the only way to go. And it does raise the level of practice. But I am also reminded of the reply given to me by a very fine bridge player when, as a comparative novitiate, I inquired after a rule for a certain situation and was told "Rules are made for morons! Play your cards!" I have never been able to transcend a concern for rules for very long, that is, I am always asking what ought to be done and why, but I can see her point and appreciate it. There is a newness and richness about experience that is often not directly interpretable by preconceived rules without irreparable loss. You need a feel for the territory as well. And this is part of the reason why Justice is blind and why we keep modifying our constraints to improve our eyesight. Therefore it is not enough merely to subordinate the acquisitive to the maintenance to fulfill our moral concern. The moral arises out of the worldliness of practice and has reference back to it for sustenance and completion. I have a great deal of respect for Spinoza's view of things *sub specie aeternitatis* but I cannot do it, literally, for the life of me. Nor does this view council turning ones back on Truth, Beauty, and Goodness. As John Herman Randall, Jr., makes so delightfully clear in his *Plato: Dramatist of the Life of Reason*, [2] if the dialogues do nothing else they show the surpassing importance of the ideal in the life and practice of mankind. Plato even has Socrates point out that one does not live in the ideal but, rather, in the light of it.[3] How to keep that light from being more than a formal glare is what this chapter, and indeed, the whole book, is all about.

As an example of how this moral concern is continuous and modified through time and change, we need only look back half a generation or so ago when, with the advent of "the pill," the opening of dormitory visiting hours and the beginning of mixed housing, many thought the younger generation was coming apart morally. When the dust settled, however, it became clear that personal integrity, sincerity and honor were just as important as ever but the limitations and constraints under which they were given meaning had changed to meet the new conditions as they emerged. In no way was this comparable to the present drug problem where a person's choice destroys the possibility of responsible practice and the person along with it. From the perspective of an ethics of practice, there are no grounds for comparing an outright evil with changing the shape of responsible practice to meet a changing world. Of course, most of these changes and the speed with which they come about are the results of human practice. Most of our ideas, and especially the moral ones because of their importance for practice, exhibit these changes through history. Nor is it easy to grant progress toward the more insightful in these matters either, as witnessed, for example, by the idea of virtue itself from its early Greek beginnings as excellence of function to its early 20th Century meaning as sexual purity.

This reaching beyond the enabling conditions as formulated in rights theory can be illustrated by the fact that we qualify rights on moral grounds in terms of the general utility of the community i.e., the need to fence property excavations to minimize harm. The whole question of individual privacy in the information age is another example and a moral as well as a legal one that will become more important as time goes on. In the Chrysler case, spoken about previously, the conservative argument was delivered as if the free market system set out certain rights, such as non-government interference, a market morality so to speak, that it would be wrong to violate and that would be destroyed or injured if Chrysler received the Government loan. The Government replied, quite correctly, that in this case the consequences of Chrysler's failure in injury to the market system far outweigh morally any injury in interfering by granting the loan. And so a new limitation was placed on condition number seven, non-interference by government in the free market in practice.

We have set out the notion of just practice i.e., when the two dimensions of practice are consistent with one another, and claimed that the categorical moral concern for practice extends beyond the conditions of the practicing self towards those of the world that practice lives in and confronts. An enlarged idea of prudence was used along with several other examples to indicate this extending beyond to include both segments of practice. Let us now restate and then move on again. In an ethics of practice, morality expresses a direct categorical concern for the inner conditions of its own possibility as against the changes in desire, interest, feeling and passion that occur in the person and also for the outer conditions of its own possibility as against the changing conditions in the world. It is this total concern for practice that our example of prudence evidences. When this balance is achieved we have a just, moral and perhaps even a successful practice. The internal conditions of the practicing self, choice, concern and consistency, can be eroded by desires, interests, feelings and passions aimed at, or in need of, particular conditions external to the self. Kant calls this heteronomous behavior as opposed to autonomous. But preserving these inner conditions is only half of the moral story. In so far as business or any other practice is only heteronomously concerned and directed to acquiring particular goals as prudently as possible, the moral dimension is lacking and practice will erode. The criterion put forward here, that a practice is right or just when it is consistent with its own possibility, was designed to insure the compatibility of such end-directed and consequential concern with the enabling conditions of autonomous practice. So far so good, and we have a basically Kantian view of the moral, one that is reasonable as far as it goes. But we have claimed that this categorical moral concern extends to the external conditions of the possibility of practice as well, to encompass multiplicity, continuity and structure.

The first thing to point out about these three external conditions is their importance for the inner three conditions. The exercise of choice, concern and consistency could not be carried out were there not multiplicity, insuring alternatives, continuity, underlying purposiveness, and structure, making choice efficacious.

It has been stated that the conditions enabling my practice are the conditions that enable anyone else to practice. My telling a lie is inconsistent with my enabling conditions and this applies to all such acts by anyone. At the same time, when I lie I am a liar but no one else is a liar or even necessarily becomes a liar as a consequence of my lying. The consequence of my lie upon the practice of someone else, however, is a falsification in the context of their practice, a result similar to a mistake being made in their context, although much more is involved if the person had reason to expect the truth. Not to check out such contextual matters whenever possible is certainly a failure in prudence and most often in moral responsibility for your own practice as well. Honesty and trust are virtues because in their absence, there can be no practice amongst persons.

Clearly, radical changes in the external conditions of practice can have radical effects upon the conditions of responsible practice. It would seem that in situations involving such radical change the corporation as an institution is subject to greater moral problems than is the individual because of the differences in their natures. Unless schizoid, individual practice is unitary, while corporate practice is by its many agents. For example, a sudden down turn in market conditions or a recession changes the conditions of organization and operation in a firm. The conditions which supported its size and practice before disappear and radical revision is required to continue. To maintain the firm and its assets, top management must take steps which it would not consider under normal conditions. All I have to do is tighten my belt, but the firm has to tighten every agent's belt. It often involves cutting back the number of employees retained and, depending upon the seriousness of the situation, such staff reductions can come about in very preemptory ways and often do not take into account the continuing well-being of those being separated. The most unprofitable operations are cut back often with little concern for the town where that firm may be a principle job source. The extreme example of this is, of course, bankruptcy when the unity of the firm dissolves into the multiplicity of its creditors.

Along with this dissolution as an entity all of its agents lose their status and also many of the accumulated benefits associated with the firm. This is surely not to the benefit of anyone involved including the firm but, due to bad management, step-motherly market changes or a combination of both, the short-term needs of survival become dominant to the exclusion of all else. Filing under Chapter 11 delays dissolution allowing time to reorganize and, if possible, to mitigate such financial and people losses. There must be a pathology of these matters and surely keeping the firm on the healthy side of these external changes is what is meant by "good management" and the test of real prudence. Just practice involves balance between the enabling conditions and the goal. When bankruptcy threatens, the conditions of survival become dominant often to the exclusion of the conditions for making and marketing the product. Practice is at odds with itself as in the pragmatic contradiction. For example, to preserve the firm and balance the poles, the union may take a cut in wages. But the opposite can occur also. Too much emphasis on the acquisitive to the exclusion of concern for the maintenance can also destroy the firm's practice. The bi-polar nature of practice requires that a just balance be kept. How do you strike this balance? Maybe you never can completely, which accounts for why Justice is blind. I often hear businessmen speak of having to choose the lesser of two evils and these situations usually arise externally. When business is good and growth and development the order of the day, you slowly extend the firm and its practice in ways that cannot be continued if times change and they always do. When talking with business people about the moral and their practice, they often look at me and ask "Have you ever had to meet a payroll?" This, of course, is a highly moral matter and subject to all the fluxuations of the market. One argument for big business is that bigness enables a greater degree of stability and staying power in the market.

The position of the new (young?) firm trying to establish itself in the market reflects these same uncertainties even to a greater degree, especially when the market is oligopolistic in character. Their survival is on the line and the pressure to succeed acquisitively encourages immoral practice. Large, established firms can and do take a longer point of view. Once again, this is no argument for the long-run as moral against the short-run as immoral.

I bring up these really obvious points in order to indicate what everyone knows: that practice is subject to changing external conditions that have a direct effect upon the possibilities for practice. Significant alteration in the alternatives presented, the established continuities and hence, on the structural possibilities available, have direct consequences for the practice of business.

Our concern for the outer conditions of practice is general in nature and takes the imperative form: "Be concerned for the consequences of external events upon the conditions of your practice!" The concern is still to keep practice consistent with its own possibility. But when outside events impinge, as they must, upon practice, the concern is to take action to preserve the possibility of practice as much as possible and this can only be done, if at all, indirectly in terms of consequences and will always take the form of an hypothetical imperative in any particular instance in the acquisitive dimension. Of course, such concern may be only partially successful or even fail completely. We will pursue this moral concern for consequences further by way of example.

In Chapter Five it was said that "...Government can encourage and support responsible practice but government can not take the place of responsible practice without undercutting its possibility." What this says is that interference from the outside in the form of consequences is not consistent with the possibility of practice. As was pointed out then, this says something about the nature of constructive regulation and the impossibility of imposing responsible practice from the outside. Return to this at this point is to emphasize that it is an instance of our categorical concern for the consequences of external actions on the conditions of practice and falls under our previously expressed criterion of right practice as being consistent with its own possibility. The decision in the Chrysler case is another example of the extension of moral concern beyond the inner conditions of the agent to the outer conditions of the world and their consequences for practice.

In the same chapter it was also said that "...the welfare state fully maintains the conditions for the exercise of responsible practice but by so doing it undercuts the significance of responsible practice itself. ...Self-fulfillment is always in response to a challenge and welfare, while it may make the challenge manageable, may also remove the challenge." To the degree to which this is so, the practice of welfare is inconsistent with its own possibility and ought not to be practiced by the community at any level. There is no moral justification for welfare as more than temporary remedy to get people back on their feet. Where it is not a restorative practice we are undercutting our possibilities as a community and our individualism is, insofar, a failure. Do not suppose, for a moment, that the concern of the ethics of practice is so narrow as to rule out compassion for the marginal in the community. Remedial welfare makes the assumption that people will respond responsibly and no other assumption is morally justified. As we pointed out in another context, that people are moral may be presumed, but where we find two or three generations on welfare, it does make one wonder. Cynicism regarding the possibility of responsible practice or adequate self-interest is never warranted for, like skepticism, it is inconsistent with its own assertion. Sometimes, of course, we are disappointed in our efforts and regret is appropriate for a practicing community or person. Spinoza's comment upon the human scene is most appropriate here:

> There is no individual thing in Nature which is not surpassed in strength and power by some other thing: but any individual thing being given, another and a stronger is also given, by which the former can be destroyed.[4]

The above is not pessimistic, just realistic about the human condition. The outer conditions of practice act as limitations upon the inner and the changes we have been speaking about indirectly effect the inner three. The moral concern extends to the consequences of such change upon the inner conditions, the shape of the world in which and against which we practice. But that the good attracts and that people will practice responsibly if given the opportunity is the only assumption worthy of consideration as consistent with the possibility of practice.

Now let us turn to the nature and foundation for the categorical "ought" in practice.

Footnotes

1. *Social Responsibilities of Business Corporations*, New York, 1971, Chapter 3, pp. 25-35.

2. New York: Columbia University Press, 1970.

3. *Republic*, Bk.V.

4. *Ethics*, Part IV, Of Human Bondage, Axiom.

Self-Reference and the Categorical in Practice

CHAPTER 8

In our continuing concern with the nature of practice and its enabling conditions, several times we have stressed that the phenomenon of self-reference is at the center of practice. In the present chapter this phenomenon will be explored and its meaning and history pointed out as context for the grounding of moral obligation and the categorical character of the enabling conditions as norms.

During the analysis of practice in Chapter Two, it was claimed that "when you reflect upon it, it seems true beyond question that there are activities, for the simple reason that the denial that there are activities is itself an activity.... It should be noted that this does not constitute a proof of activity, but it does cut the ground from under the opposition in the same way the skeptic is silenced."

To complete the comparison, the skeptic is making a claim to knowledge when he denies that knowledge is possible or claims there is no knowledge. The ground is cut from under the claim by the assertion of the claim. The skeptic, if he is to remain a skeptic, must be silent on pain of destroying his own position. And so it is with anyone wishing to deny there are activities of the kind we have been talking about. The assertion of the claim has all the marks the claim asserted denies.

But just because you cannot assert either denial, "There is no knowledge!" or "There is no activity!," without being involved in a pragmatic contradiction that is self-refuting, it does not follow, as it would from a logical contradiction, that either of the claims that "there is knowledge!" or that "there is activity!" is necessarily true. From a logical contradiction it would follow that if you can show that the assumption "p is not round" implies a contradiction (that is, "p is both round and not round"), then "p must be round." This is one of the strongest and most ancient arguments against an opponent, the *reductio ad absurdum.* But the pragmatic contradiction doesn't work that way. The self-refuting aspect arises through an irreducible conflict between the poles of activity, a conflict of means and ends. In both instances the intent is to deny something and the means used nullify that intent; the end chosen in both cases is nullified by the means necessary to achieve it. Historically, this self-refuting aspect is perhaps best exemplified in the famous ancient paradox "Epimenides the Cretan said that all Cretans are liars." If what Epimenides said is false the whole statement is true and if what he said is true, the whole is false.

This ancient paradox of Epimenides is in a different form as a statement than our previous examples of pragmatic contradiction, i.e., the assertions "There is no knowledge!" and "There are no activities!" The latter could be restated as "Practice is impossible!" but the result remains, the assertion, indicated by quotation marks, is at odds with the content of the assertion. Both standpoints are contained in the statement about Epimenides and there is no problem with asserting it, but the two standpoints undercut each other. Another example of this conflict of standpoints, very old but still comic, has a person inquire loudly, "Is anybody here?" and the answer comes back "No!" These are often called the paradoxes of self-reference and result from the relation of practice to itself. This is a practical perspective and not a theoretical one. In the last analysis, the theoretical employment of reason presupposes the practical employment of reason and the former can only be justified by reference to the enabling conditions of practical reason.

Looked at in the light of practice, of purposive activity, however, the upshot of pragmatic contradiction is that not all things are permitted. In all of the examples above, the conditions of assertion preclude certain ends from being chosen as self-stultifying. This doesn't mean, of course, that you can't choose these ends and assert them, but the existential posture of the assertion in relation to the idea being claimed as the case produces nonsense. The norms of practice can be talked about in hypothetical fashion, but the only way to grasp their categorical nature as norms is to see for yourself. As I will try to make clear, the foundations of the sense of obligation without which responsibility has little meaning rest upon this self-referential aspect of practice.

The phenomenon of self-reference which lies at the very center of practice may be described as the capacity to be an object for yourself, or, more simply put, as the fact that we are aware we are aware, the self-consciousness that is part of human consciousness. Whether in fact, all consciousness exhibits this double aspect of being aware you are aware is an interesting question—one which I am inclined to answer in the affirmative, though not without recognizing differing degrees or levels of such development—but that it is a feature of human consciousness does not appear open to dispute. Indeed, the rock of self-awareness and self-knowledge is the principal part of the foundation of modern thought. Moreover, it is the centrality of this phenomenon that distinguishes modern thought most clearly from that of the ancients and medievals. Of course, as far back as Plato's *Theatetus* we find the idea that knowledge is distinguished from opinion by virtue of knowing that you know, that is, understanding that the object known *must* be the way it is and not some other way. Rene Descartes (1596-1650), the generally acknowledged father of modern thought, councils us not to accept anything as true "unless it presents itself so clearly and distinctly to my mind that there is no reason or occasion to doubt it"[1] And this condition tends to be the case wherever the deductive relation between premises and conclusion is seen to hold. This procedure rests the whole matter on the status of the premises and produces only hypothetical certainty (If P then C) unless the premises are seen to be so, necessarily. But this employment as the criterion of knowledge only makes use of self-reference without bringing out its basic nature.

The nub of the phenomenon of self-reference comes into view first in Plato's *Apology* (21d-23b) where Socrates, in his defense before the Athenian court, argues that he differs from other men only in that he knows he doesn't know. This is certainly an instance of the notion of knowledge in the *Theaetetus* mentioned before. But it is couched in negative terms, Socrates knows he does not know. As he reflects upon the various answers given him by those to whom he has asked the question "What is virtue?," he recognizes that all are inadequate and he knows he doesn't have the answer. This, of course, is something he knows for certain. The same kind of conclusion is implicit at the end of the *Theaetetus*. Three proposed definitions of knowledge have been advanced and found wanting, one after the other. The participants in the dialogue conclude they do not know what knowledge is and the dialogue ends. Implicitly, however, and ironically, they know they do not know. This is the conclusion, explicitly, in the *Apology*. So far as I can discover these are the only two places in Plato where the definition of the *Theaetetus*, knowing that you know, is satisfied.

It is significant that both instances are negative. Both reflect upon the activities of answering the question at hand and, finding all answers wanting in some respect, they conclude they know they do not know. A legitimate goal is set and criteria are worked out and applied by Socrates, in both instances, that show their attempts to attain the goal to be inadequate. This they know for sure. It is, of course, a truism that the knowledge claims of science are most assured when it proceeds lobster-like and by exclusion. The two examples of knowledge in Plato are of self-certainty that one must see for oneself and they revolve about the phenomenon of self-reference in a context of purposive practice. One can conclude the denial of the end of an activity with certainty provided one knows the marks of the end. It becomes ironic when the end chosen is knowledge, in that the certainty of denying the end, having knowledge of that end, affirms knowledge about it.

Usually the Platonic dialectic, the question and answer method employed most often by Socrates, is thought to lead to knowledge and the knowledge itself as being the result of illumination, a kind of jump beyond (the spark generated by rubbing the teacher and pupil together in the *7th Letter*), but the criteria of knowledge put forth in *Theaetetus* can only be fulfilled within the context of practice where the phenomenon of self-reference is present. In such dialectical illumination, what is disclosed is not so much a self-standing item of objective knowledge to be added to ones store as it is a function of the context that brought about the disclosure. This is certainly the case in the experimental sciences where practice has been institutionalized and where only a sharable and repeatable dialectic invests any disclosure with significance. On a more mundane level, it often happens that in the morning, after a good discussion with friends, the conviction of the importance of things said remains but the dialectical context with its particular torque and twist is gone and so is the illumination it fostered. These considerations also reflect the importance of argument or method in the broadest terms in all varieties of practice.

The negative quality of the examples in Plato raises the question whether there are any positive examples. As far as I know, the first use in a positive way occurs in the *Confessions* of Augustine with his argument for the undeniable fact of Self upon which knowledge of God is erected (the characterization of this by Wilhelm Windelband (1848-1915), the German philosopher and historian, as "the metaphysics of inner experience" is completely happy) and then later and more sweepingly in Descartes as the undeniable stopping-point of his methodological doubting, the famous *Cogito Ergo Sum*. As Descartes puts it:

> But then I immediately realized that while I was thinking of everything as false, I, who was so thinking, necessarily had to be something. Noting that this truth: *I think therefore I am*, was so firm and assured that all of the most extravagant supposition of the skeptics were incapable of shaking it....[2]

The certainty claimed for the *Cogito* does not rest upon some deductive or immediately intuited relation between premises and conclusion. If it did the certainty of the *Cogito* would rest upon theoretical grounds. A good case can be made that Descartes, at least sometimes, thought of it in this fashion. Rather, the certainty of the *Cogito* resides in the peculiar relation which an activity performed by a self-conscious being has to itself, namely, that in being "aware of" it is impossible to deny the "awareness" even though you may question what you are aware of.

Here in the *Cogito* we have in a simple and more general form the essential condition found in the first example discussed. Instead of the pragmatic contradiction which the denial of activity produced, in the *Cogito* the result is that the activity of doubting, which intends some end being doubted, not only cannot be doubted, but is actually affirmed in the doubting of that end. The affirmation is a disclosure of self-awareness, the being of the activity cannot be doubted by one engaged in it. And, as we have previously noted, the activity engaged in presupposes a self or agent in the limited and specific sense required by practice.

Elsewhere,[3] I have argued that whether you should interpret this self-certifying awareness on an "agent-action" or a "process-product" model is not clear from the activity itself. Indeed, there are grounds for supposing both are required to make human behavior intelligible. However, the certainty does not attach to the interpretation but to the activity itself, and it is this self-certainty that is the centerpoint of practice. Perhaps the choice of the phrase "self-certainty" is somewhat infelicitous because I do not intend to make any capital out of the supposed disclosure through the *Cogito* either of a self or of the certainty of its existence. What is to be made of this reflective experience is as much a matter of interpretation as is what is to be made of the world around us. Nor is the certainty involved of the kind producing general truth. Both Augustine and Descartes, as well as Locke, thought to use this self-certainty as a first item in their systems of theoretical knowledge, but I think the attempts were failures. They were failures because the certainty in the *Cogito* is neither certainty about the "what" of something nor the certainty of a necessary relation between ideas. A look at the salient features of that activity of which the *Cogito* is the expression will show its lack of qualifications to be called knowledge in any usual sense. (The following three points are to be found in Professor Hintikka's article "*Cogito Ergo Sum*: *Inference or Performance*."[4] The uses of the three and the fourth which follows them, however, remain my own.)

The *Cogito* is characterized by: (1) its particularity - the connection of the activity (doubting) and the indubitability of existence is present only for the person performing the activity; (2) its non-generalizability—it can never serve as the basis for an inference that all thinking involves existence; (3) its momentariness—the indubitability of existence lasts only so long as the activity performed. Another should be added, (4) its indubitability—which arises from that peculiar relation which self- conscious activity has to itself. Certainly, it was the indubitability of the situation expressed in the *Cogito* for Descartes that suggested something upon which to found the structure of certain knowledge. He did not see, however, that this indubitability arises in and has reference only to practice.

In the light of our previous analysis of activity these first three characteristics need commentary. The fourth will be dealt with separately, later on.

(1) As is the case with all the examples we have looked at, the disclosure of the *Cogito* is particular—present only to the person carrying out the activity. This does not mean that all persons engaged in activity will or must be aware of it, but it is there for the reflective taking, so to speak, and can be seen. There is an important point relevant to the foundations of responsibility here because, as with the disclosure of the *Cogito*, the grounds of responsibility are there even if you do not happen to be aware of them.

(2) The disclosure of the *Cogito* may not be the basis for a generalization such as "all thinking involves existence," but that depends upon how you are to understand "thinking involves existence." It may mean that thinking involves an object; all thinking is about something, but because I am thinking about Atlantis does not imply that there is such a place. It may mean that thinking presupposes the limited self spoken of before. Thinking is an activity and one of the conditions, without which not, is a self, continuous throughout the activity and identical with itself. One can say: if there is activity then this limited notion of the self is presupposed, but that is only hypothetical. However, being engaged in the activity and reflecting upon it, the necessity of this self is disclosed. It may be that the disclosure and its meaning cannot be generalized—the generalization would be hypothetical and the felt necessity would vanish. But even though the disclosed necessity is for me, I think that from the very nature of the disclosure it makes sense to expect that anyone reflecting upon an engaged-in activity could have the same disclosure and that includes myself five minutes from now. But, once the disclosure occurs, I then know something meaningful about activity: that it presupposes a self. Even though the disclosure is particular in the sense that it occurs to me, it is still intelligible in the sense that disclosures disclose something.

(3) The third point—that the indubitability is momentary and lasts only as long as the activity persists—is well taken. The existential necessity is contextual and should the context collapse so would the disclosure. The term "momentary," however, is bothersome, for activity, be it ever so short, requires duration to realize the end aimed at. If you think of the disclosure of the *Cogito* and the context of that disclosure in separate and isolated terms, then the fact that the necessity disclosed is dependent upon the particular context of the *Cogito* might tend to make the term "momentary" appropriate. But viewing the *Cogito* as an instance of activity as we have described it, the tendency is to think of activity as the locus of the truly human, even as the framework of intelligibility. The suggestion would be that the conditions of activity are the conditions of being a person. While one activity may cease or be terminated and another begun, the development and maintenance of the conditions of activity is a very enlightening way to think about the human enterprise as such. In this sense there is nothing momentary about the disclosure of the *Cogito* at all.

I am not, of course, maintaining that self-reference expresses itself in all practice as we find it in the *Cogito*. Most of the time purposive activity can be carried out with only those aspects of self-reference needed for judgment and control. But there are certain contexts, let me borrow an existentialist term and call them "boundary" situations, when the fact of self-reference becomes central. And in these boundary situations the fact of self-reference generates an awareness of certain limitations functioning as imperatives for and constraints upon practice.

If the indubitability of the *Cogito* and, by extension, the rest of these boundary situations, is neither the certainty of the "what" of something nor the necessity of the implication relation between ideas, then what kind of necessity is it? It is not logical necessity because one of the terms of the relation is an existing event, the activity. Clearly the activity is intelligible and may involve a wide range of concepts between some of which logical relations may obtain. In so far as this necessity is not conceptual it is not expressible or conveyable by propositions. It is not certifiable by reference to meaning alone. I am inclined to characterize it as an existential necessity of practice arising from the self-referential relation conscious practice has to itself. Further, this necessity is unconditioned.

To refer to this necessity as unconditioned raises the question whether there is such. From the theoretical point of view, amongst our ideas, there is only conditioned necessity of an hypothetical sort such that something being given, something else must be so. From the point of view of practice, however, the situation is different. Previously, in considering freedom of choice as a presupposition of purposive activity, it was said that the past must be an item for me in the present and not just the set of preconditions of which the present is the expression, if there is to be choice. The necessities of practice do not derive from conditions prior to practice but arise out of our capacity to initiate action and our awareness of doing so. This is what I take Kant to mean when he speaks of the will as giving a law to itself as the basis for its own activity. This is the root of the categoricalness of Kant's imperative. The three laws of thought referred to in Chapter Two are one of the clearest and most easily grasped examples of this necessity of practice. Recognition of the necessity arises out of reflecting upon those conditions without which such activity could be neither initiated nor sustained. And the normative character of them arises out of our awareness that we are free not to follow them. But how does the recognition of this necessity come about?

The first requirement is that there be something to reflect upon, that is, a purposive activity must be in progress. Now, it is quite possible to be so completely involved in what you are doing that you are not reflectively aware of just what you are doing i.e., being so engrossed in your work you do not realize it is growing too dark to work until someone turns the light on for you. You are busy with execution and busy applying standards needed for judging the progress of your performance. Often such execution requires the application of a skill acquired through practice. Not only can your doing be under your control, as is the case in purposive behavior, but your controlling can be reflected upon in the light of your doing.

It is in practice that the conditions of and the need for self-government arise. If I were self-sufficient instead of finite, activity would be unnecessary. If I could acquire what I require with no risk to myself, except in so far as I might be mistaken about what would be good or useful if acquired, then action would be very straightforward, if sometimes mistaken. But in fact activity can be self-destructive. We spoke of "boundary" conditions earlier as expressive of this possibility. The phrase "self-government," then, is not just a political condition but is descriptive of that capacity in man to carry on reasoned, responsible activity.

In this chapter the importance of self-reference to practice and the way in which it is the source of the limitations upon purposive activity have been considered. Now, we must return to the status of the moral imperative previously labelled categorical and unconditioned but left without full explanation. And at this point we pick up the commentary on the *Cogito*, point (4), its indubitability.

So far I have been laying out the class conditions of purposive activity and responsible practice, have pointed out the presuppositions which are normative for the class and have taken membership in this class as the locus of responsibility. But the question remains: "What makes the enabling conditions of purposive activity obligatory and categorical for the individual?" Would not such obligation impinge only upon the members of the class and be considered hypothetical only and not categorical for each or any individual? As pointed out before, you can get out from under the "ought" of an hypothetical imperative merely by denying the antecedent condition upon which the "ought" depends. But if you attempt to treat this as an hypothetical imperative of the form "If you want to carry on purposive activity, then you ought to preserve the conditions enabling it," and then deny the if-clause with "but I don't want to carry on purposive activity," you are caught in the same way the skeptic who denies there is any knowledge and the person who denies there is activity are caught—the assertion of your denial cuts the ground out from under the content of your denial. This is not a theoretical proof; there can be none by the nature of the case. But it is a practical proof. In so far as human beings carry on purposive activity and I would maintain that such activity is descriptive of as well as prescriptive for the peculiarly human, these norms apply to what humans do. I recognize this existential "ought" as categorical and unconditionally binding upon my own practice and this obligation can be seen to apply by anyone *so engaged* if they will reflect upon the conditions of their own engagement. This obligation arises from my recognition that in the existential context of practice, I am categorically committed to these conditions, my doing presupposes them. I am able to do otherwise, but I "ought" not to because they are the conditions of my own being as a free, responsible person. The categoricalness of these norms is reflective in nature, that is, my being engaged in practice as I am now presupposes these norms as the conditions of my doing, of my being able to practice as a fully responsible person.

This obligation can only be recognized by the practicing individual. Argument by anyone else is only hypothetical, but for me it can be seen as categorically binding. Knowledge of the nature of the activity I am engaged in is certainly derived from experience, but knowledge of the norms governing that experienced activity is arrived at by reflection upon the enabling conditions of activity. Such knowledge is based upon experience but not derived from experience. This is what I take Kant to mean when he says ethical principles are *a priori* and not empirical. While that action is permitted which is universalizable, the recognition of this obligation has nothing to do with the universality of the conditions for they apply to the class. It is mainly for this reason—because it centers on this self-referential aspect of practice— that I have chosen "consistent with its own possibility" as basic moral criterion instead of any other possible formulation.

To repeat, because this is so central; the normativeness of the enabling conditions is recognized through reflection and grounded in the phenomenon of self-reference and it comes with the recognition of my necessary inclusion as a person under the class-conditions of purposive activity.

Reflective beings discover the moral as grounded in their experience in the sense that the neglect of it destroys the human capacity for it and yet in so far as they act in the light of this discovery in the many and varying facets of their practice, they create and sustain something that would not be without them and in so doing they create and sustain themselves as free and responsible persons as well. I believe it is this condition which Kant refers to as "respect for the moral law." We are all involved in maintaining the conditions of responsible personhood for ourselves as well as others. It would seem that this is the primary and supportive relationship of members of a community to each other and to themselves.

It is quite simple to think about the nature of practice as was done in the earlier chapters and to come up with its essential characteristics and the conditions which must be present in order for practice to be possible. But from that standpoint there is nothing categorically binding or necessary about either practice or its enabling conditions. However, if we step inside of practice — and that is the importance of having said several times that only within the context of practice, only in the midst of practice, does the moral arise, — then the enabling conditions take on their categorically normative functions as moral "oughts." Theirs is a reflective certainty, the only one I know of, grounded in the phenomenon of self-reference. Of course, this certainty by itself does not constitute the moral. The condition of choice and the universality of these enabling conditions for all practice coupled with the categoricalness of this imperative for practice constitute the foundations for the sense of obligation and the moral "ought."

Footnotes

1. "Discourse on Method," *Essential Works of Descartes*, Part II, New York: Bantam Books, 1966, p. 12.

2. Ibid., Part 2, p. 20.

3. *Cartesian Essays*, The Hague: M. Nijhoff, 1969, p. 65.

4. *Meta-Meditations: Studies in Descartes*, A. Sesonske and N. Fleming, eds., Belmont, Calif.: Wadsworth Publishing Company, 1965, pp. 50ff.

Corporate Character

CHAPTER 9

In this chapter we shall consider in what sense, if any, moral responsibility can be assigned to the corporation. The analogy between the individual person and the corporation will continue to be taken seriously as the basis for an organic view of corporate practice and for moral judgment.

As I read and reflect upon the current attempts to affirm or deny the applicability of the moral to the corporation, the key argument in the negative seems to be that one can only be held morally responsible for what one does or does not do and since corporations, as entities, never do or fail to do anything—in fact, they employ persons to do for them—they cannot be held morally responsible. Legally, they are held responsible for what their agents do or do not do for them, but that is a different matter entirely and as a fact hardly a basis for moral judgment. On the face of it, there doesn't seem to be any way around the conclusion of this argument and it reflects certainly one very basic sense in which corporations are not like persons; they cannot initiate action. All of which makes it difficult to connect ethics and moral judgment to corporate practice unless we ignore the corporate level and reduce corporate practice to the multiplicity of individual agents acting for the corporation. Then, there would be an aggregate of personal acts, some broader and some narrower in scope, with the broader including by direction many of the narrower much as an onion is organized. Taken all together, these would constitute the corporate level of activity and to say "The corporation did so and so" would be an *omnium gatherum* way of speaking, saying nothing at all about the action of any corporate entity.

There surely is some truth to this approach and it, no doubt, raises problems of its own not the least of which is the traditional "corporate veil" behind which, in practice, the individual agent is shielded from the consequences of his actions in the name of the corporation. But such a reduction seems to be inherently unsatisfactory because this conception denies to the corporation exactly that element which the onion alluded to before obviously has, a unity and status of its own and, hence, of importance morally. Such a denial tends to weaken, if not destroy, the sense of responsibility. I believe there is another approach to this whole matter which can locate a sense of moral responsibility applicable to the corporate level of activity without running afoul of the key argument set forth above. If such a sense could be established, it would not only anchor moral judgment at the corporate level but aid us in thinking about certain moral aspects of corporate governance.

In the first place, to repeat, insofar as moral responsibility rests upon judgments of activity as right or wrong, no corporation can be held morally responsible because, quite simply, corporations don't do anything. But now we must ask whether judgments of activity are the only kind of moral judgments we make. The answer is no; we also make moral judgments of character. For example, as the poet says, "King John was not a good man, he had his little ways..." Judgments of character are made in terms of "good" and "bad" rather than "right" and "wrong" but they are closely related to judgments of activity. King John was not a good man because we could expect his "little ways" to turn up in his behavior and, as the poet goes on to say, "Sometimes no one spoke to him for days and days and days." We recognize the close relationship between activity and the conditions fostering it and out of which it arises and we make moral judgments about those conditions as being either good or bad. When young and having done something wrong I remember being told I was a bad boy and then treated as such in the hope I would "mend my ways" before it was too late; activity stems from and reflects character and character shepherds action. Fagan in *Oliver Twist* is a man of bad character because of his influence upon the youngsters he employs and Iago is, in a way, the paragon of pure evil for we can find no good reason for his betrayal of Othello. However, judgments of character apply not only to persons but to places and things. Sodom and Gommorah are judged to be "moral abominations" in the Good Book and it is not uncommon for parents to have moral objections to their children hanging-around the local bar. What is being judged here? It is not only the presence of corrupt practice that is being judged although that constitutes a part of the evidence for such judgement. It is, rather, the pervasiveness and dominance of such practice and to such a degree that we judge the young man from the country to have no chance at all in Sin City. One way or another and perhaps every way he turns he will be corrupted. Judgments of character are concerned with the presence or absence of conditions fostering right, or what used to be called virtuous, activities and we make the same judgments about persons and even things as we make about places.

If the moral dimension of human concern were self-standing and unrelated to the context of events, then we could be satisfied with confining moral judgments to individual actions. But as this is patently not the case it makes sense to recognize the extension of moral concern and judgment to the conditions which enhance or reduce the possibility of moral activity. Clearly, to make such judgment is not to blame an individual because we know the place or group is not a person, but since we also know that the character of such a group or place is largely constituted by the principles and practices of persons, such judgment speaks to the locus of responsibility, the place or group itself. From this perspective, a morally bad corporation is one from whom morally wrong practice can be expected. And, since corporate character is the concern of management, moral responsibility for wrong practice belongs directly to management in both senses of commission and omission. As mentioned previously, the law is only slowly coming to reflect this fact with the gradual removal of the "corporate veil." Clearly, this is one of the basic areas of business practice where "rugged individualism" and its protection is being civilized to meet current needs and pressures. There can be little doubt about whether our local bars offer satisfactory conditions of nurture for our young and Fagan was raising a pack of thieves and pickpockets. Upon reflection, it occurs to me that my reference to the Bible as the Good Book a few moments ago is an instance of the type of moral judgments of which I am speaking. Of course, there are other "good books" in this moral sense too. We use "good" in other ways but the moral usage of "good" in judging the character of persons, places and things refers to the supporting conditions, or what I have called the enabling conditions of responsible practice.

Corporations and businesses have this same dimension of character as the ground and foundation from which actions are initiated and I suggest that such moral judgments of character can be meaningfully and appropriately applied to corporations. Some businesses have good character and some, like King John, have their "little ways." We speak of Company X as "a good place to work" or Company Y as "a bad outfit to do business with" and the reference is unmistakably to the conditions obtaining in these companies, to their character.

Any member of a management team at no matter what level of an organization has to be concerned not only with the doing of certain activities but with the character and the quality of the doing involved. And, of course, the responsibility for the character and integrity of the operation increases as you ascend the corporate ladder. But at bottom even the traditional concern of business for efficiency in production is a concern for character. The problem with that approach arose from the application of a mechanical model of efficiency to the human context and resulted in the inefficient use of human resources at the very least, not to mention the effects upon the person so involved. Our continuing contemporary concern with codes of ethics as part of making explicit the operating procedures of a business is a concern for character brought about by the need for careful self-regulation of decision procedures lest in their absence such regulation be imposed from the outside. Whatever the difficulties with our present regulatory climate may be, one lasting benefit seems to be that all businesses have become more reflective and self-conscious about the human dimension of their operations and for reasons more basic than, and not only confined to, public relations. In their excellent little book, *Ethics and Profits*, Leonard Silk and David Vogel suggest that the problem of the legitimacy of corporate power in our society can best be answered, and the public given the needed assurance, by the institution of moral principles of corporate conduct by top management along with the needed follow-up to make them stick. This is clearly a concern for corporate character as the condition for action.

Many times the moral character of the founder of a company comes to be part of the character of the company itself long after he has departed. Also, when there is trouble in a firm, top management is often replaced not only to forestall further trouble but to change the character of the whole operation. The reciprocity between character and action is as important for the corporation as it is for the individual. And it is just in this concern for character and its relation to action that our analogy between the person and the corporation finds a most positive, similar and suggestive grounding. It used to be thought that if you had been properly habituated, that is, had developed the proper virtues, your actions would be an expression of them, but in our time, what with rapid change and diversification of function, self-conscious action in the light of operational principles has come to be the model of decision procedures. It is neither safe nor sensible to be your own criteria in the complexity of the modern firm. Perhaps it never was although you could get away with it more easily in the past.[1] Let us look at this relation between character and action more closely.

It is not easy to state the complex relation of character to action on the level of the individual. It is certainly true to say that action is expressive of individual character, but in so saying we are speaking of a quality of the action rather than the aim of the action and the quality is expressive of the character of the agent; the quality of tolerance or sincerity possessed by an action, no matter what its end may be, is expressive of the dispositional property trait of tolerance or sincerity. And this indicates that character has more than just a simple cause and effect relation to action. No doubt in a given instance my goal may be to be tolerant or sincere, but more often it is the case that no matter what my particular goal may be my action will exhibit the quality of tolerance or sincerity because, no matter what else it may do, it does not transgress or violate the operational criteria I have for tolerance and sincerity. This means that character surrounds action and from the point of view of practice is more often a set of limitations restraining or shaping actions in certain ways than it is a simple matter of expression. Action occurs within the context of character and, as I said before, is shepherded by character. Perhaps a mother's love for her infant is shepherding in this way, at first rather simple and a straightforward response to perceived needs, but then reflected upon and expressed in certain operational guidelines for infant care. A good mother surrounds her infant and takes the place of the character it does not yet have. Hopefully, it will grow up with its own character and be the self-governing individual our democratic system presupposes of its members.

In the case of the individual, the character and the action are rooted in the same source, but in the case of the corporation this connection does not exist. Of course, the best thing to do is to hire good people and that is exactly what we do when we hire people qualified to do the job to be done. But then we talk about a good cook or a good manager and not a good person. When businesses were small, one good person, in all the relevant senses of "good" including the moral, could mother a whole enterprise, could combine character and action for the benefit of the company. That is exactly what the fabled entrepreneur does so well. But as anyone knows who has shepherded an enterprise from its beginnings, there comes a time when you can't do everything, the requirements of action go beyond your care and control, beyond the individual limits of your own character. And this is where character and action become separate. In the large contemporary corporation this separation is multiplied thousands of times. We protect the company and ourselves with respect to the actions we expect a new person to take by having detailed job descriptions. But with respect to character we assume it to be good unless the recommendations indicate otherwise and we tell the new person that in a short time he will get the hang of how things are done. It is just this gap between character and action that policy directives and the codes of ethics mentioned earlier come into being to remedy. Not that we can close the gap by issuing directives. It cannot be bridged. By making character explicit in the form of principles as guides and limits for action, we establish a common company character and endow the multiplicity of actions taken in its name with common qualities.

These common qualities which are continuous throughout the operation of the business become the character of the business we carry on, the criteria in the light of which it operates. Such character often grows like Topsy because the actions of every person working for the company will exhibit qualities of character, of his or her shepherding, and some of these qualities will be more appropriate than others. This is undoubtedly why the traditional emphasis upon company purpose and loyalty has grown up as a unifying dimension for the actions of all managers taking the place of a wide range of character traits expressive of individual interest. And it is because the company has most often been understood as an instrument for the profit of its owners that company interest has been formulated almost exclusively in terms of its instrumental, end-oriented operations. But contemporary corporations are hardly instrumental in only that narrow sense. The classical view that an executive's only responsibility is to return a profit to the shareholder-owners has been commented on previously. Contemporary corporate management seeks to secure and maintain, through growth and development, the institution it shepherds. This means fulfilling a whole range of obligations to its essential constituencies, among which are included a decent return on investment, and carrying out the actions needed to produce and market its goods or services. But it also means maintaining the needed traits of corporate character—everything from efficiency, dealing with the relations of means to ends, to honesty, dealing with the various facets of the relationships of persons to persons and company to persons, to integrity, dealing with a firm's viability as an institution. Top management is responsible both for the actions of its agents and for the character of the firm. We make moral judgments of activity about the former assignable to the agents and we make moral judgments of character about the latter assignable to the corporation itself as the place, the context of principles and criteria (virtues) surrounding and shepherding all company activity.

So far I have set out a notion of corporate character and the moral judgment of it on analogy with the individual character of persons. We judge a person's character as morally good or bad. We hold persons morally responsible for their actions as right or wrong, however, we do not hold a person morally responsible for his character. But character and action are so closely connected that the last statement about a person not being responsible for his character would not hold except in so far as by character or disposition we meant something like habit. We would not hold a congenital liar responsible for his lie; he can not do otherwise. Yet, I have the capacity to lie and I ought not to exercise it. It is choice that makes the difference. Without certain capacities I couldn't be a morally responsible person and I might acquire certain habits that would block off those capacities. The traditional notion of virtue meant excellence of function which explains the character in terms of the action. All of the moral virtues are perfected capacities, but not all perfected capacities are moral virtues. And once we get into perfected capacities, such as rational, honest, reliable, responsible or sincere, character and action seem to be continuous in one sense and yet in another sense, reciprocal, in that character influences action and action influences character. The moral aspects of character in persons center about these perfected capacities. Corporations, however, do not have any capacities at all, hence both the need to engage the capacities of persons as agents and the gap in corporate being between character and action. It is important to discover in what ways, if at all, we can think of the corporation in moral terms because unless our institutions reflect our values, our values will be destroyed.

It is just because of the gap between character and action at the corporate level, just because every action is taken for a corporation by an agent, that the claim by Peter French, in his article "The Corporation as Moral Person," goes too far. He holds "that corporations should be treated as full-fledged moral persons and hence that they can have whatever privileges, rights and duties as are, in the normal course of affairs, accorded to moral persons."[2] It is an interesting conception much of which is suggestive and makes good sense but I don't think it will go where Professor French takes it. Let me see if I can say why it will not.

There are three pieces on the game board: a person who can act, the same person as agent for the corporation (let us say, as president) and the corporation as constituted by its Corporate Internal Decision Structure, French's CID, (a part of what I have been calling "corporate character"). Certainly this CID not only sets forth what it means to be a particular kind of agent (the president of this corporation as well as for all other positions), but it also sets forth the framework of purposes, intentions and relationships prescribing and describing legitimate action for the corporation by the person as president. Certainly, as French does, we can distinguish the reasons of the person for that action from the reasons of the person as president for that action and both of these from the reasons or policies set forth in the CID governing presidential action. No doubt, all three may be the same and all three may be different. But though there are three levels of intention indicated, the question comes down to whether you can ascribe it to the person as individual and the person as president. It would seem that you cannot. In the first place, to the objection that "corporate policies reflect only the current goals of its directors," French objects that this is neither logically necessary nor in fact the case.[3] Of course, this is true, the point being that our person as president is more often subject to the CID than he is a creator of it. But while it is true that the president is subject to the CID there is also a real sense in which there is no CID unless there are duly elected corporate officers who sustain it. Perhaps my point will be clearer by reference to the legal conditions required for bringing a corporation into being. Not only must there be a CID including the corporate offices but there must be duly constituted persons filling those corporate offices or there is no corporation. The CID by itself is only a formal structure, not a corporation. The suggestion is not that the moral should follow the legal, but that the legal has followed the moral as it so often does. Professor French's argument for the moral personhood of the corporation is made more plausible through his use of an analogy with game theory.[4] It goes like this: just as the rules of baseball are constitutive of the game of baseball so the CID of the corporation is constitutive of the corporation.

This kind of argument brings up very fundamental problems. It appears to give status to all conceivable games, for instance, whether anyone ever played them or not. Essences with or without instances point in the direction of a realm of something like Platonic forms and I bring this up here because I cannot tell, from what French says, whether the CID which he takes to have status as a moral person is just a set of rules, as his game analogy suggests, of positions and relations, such as what a president is and what he may or must do, without any instances, or whether, in fashion reminiscent of Neo-Platonism, along with the rule for presidents, a president is included. The game analogy leans me toward the former but when he says that "corporations are collectivities,"[5] he seems to mean that a corporation is a collection of individuals unified by common purpose. The former view falls on the side of what has been called "character" and of the formal nature of the corporation while the latter neatly bridges the gap between character and action combining the rule with the instance, essence with existence in traditional terms, the concept of a president with a president in our example, the way it is in persons. In sum, I don't believe the game theory analogy leads to the idea of a collectivity unless founded on some variety of atomism.

I mention atomism here not because French's position is taken to be one but because "collectivity" sounds atomistic, a group of things unified without indicating the principle of unification, and on the game analogy different rules make different entities. Our problem is to understand *how* what we, as rational organisms, as persons, have created i.e., the corporation as an extension of our own interests and purposes,— to understand *how* what we have created *can* reflect the open-ended rationality that we, at our best, are able to bring to our practice. As we said earlier, this corporation we have created has no capacities. It is totally dependent upon the capacities of its agents for all its action. And the basic capacity that enables its agents to act for a corporation is the ability to have something other than itself or some function other than its own as an object of concern for itself. The concern belongs to the agent but it is the object of concern that counts. Earlier, the love of a mother for her child was an example of this ability. The mother may not in fact know what is good for the child or her emotions may cloud her vision of what is needed, but the concern is for the child. When on a cold morning I need to start my car to get to work I had better forget about everything else and concentrate on how to start my car in cold weather. I had better become the proper instrument for realizing that goal if the car is ever to function instrumentally in relation to my goals. As St. Paul put it, in order to save yourself you must lose yourself. Without this capacity we could be full of desire or need and never be satisfied except by chance. On this capacity rests human purposiveness and intentionality. What Professor French calls the CID and what I have called corporate character is the network of goals, principles and procedures as object of concern for the agents filling the positions of the corporation.

You can certainly say that a corporate agent has a responsible character, one that will carry out company directives, and that he can be trusted and counted on to do so. But does it make sense to say that a corporation has a responsible character? I think it does! Earlier, in saying "it makes sense to recognize the extension of moral concern and judgment to the conditions which enhance or reduce the possibility of moral activity," my intent was to point out a relation between character and action, in this case, the character of the corporation and the action of its agents. Further, it was said that "judgments of character are concerned with the presence or absence of conditions fostering right... activities," and that "the moral usage of 'good' in judging the character of persons, places and things refers to the supporting conditions or what I have called the enabling conditions of responsible practice." Good character shepherds right action. If this makes sense, then what conditions of corporate character distinguish between the morally good and the morally bad? Certainly, a large part of a good corporate character would consist of the conditions proper to fulfillment of its policies and purposes and, since persons as agents must do everything that is to be done in this connection, some portion of these corporate conditions must include those insuring that their agents can and do give their very best as responsible persons in their action for the corporation. This is especially important, indeed imperative, in times of rapid change and differing conditions. In the grip of change, corporate casuistry won't work any better than human casuistry does and the classification of recognizable instances under known rules becomes increasingly difficult. Only human, open-ended rationality, human nature at its best, has the capacity to adapt, innovate and preserve itself. But this concern for maintaining and even fostering the conditions for responsible practice in its agents is not imperative only because of changing conditions or only because it will further corporate purposes. Those are good reasons but, as I have been trying to show here, it is imperative under all conditions of practice because the freedom of choice exercised in an agent's action carries with it the possibility of destroying those conditions and, therefore, that capacity for the agent and for everyone effected by the action. This possibility is resident in all action and constitutes the moral imperative for all human practice. To this way of thinking, that act is moral which is consistent with its own possibility. Whatever else an act might do, it would maintain its own enabling conditions. Good corporate character can foster and promote, even require, optimum conditions for human practice to the benefit of everyone. If this sounds like an appeal from the Better Business Bureau, it isn't. But it is the most adequate foundation for that worthy effort.

Such corporate character would exhibit moral responsibility in the third sense distinguished by Professor Goodpaster in his paper in the *Journal of Business Ethics* entitled "The Concept of Corporate Responsibility."[6] Speaking of the third sense, the "decision making sense of the word" responsible, he writes:

> When we say of Bill Jones that he is a responsible person we convey that he is reliable and trustworthy, that he can be depended upon to interpret situations and take actions that manifest both integrity and concern for those affected by them. The emphasis is not on Bill Jones as the agent who brought about a certain result (the causal sense), on his following rules or role-expectations (the rule-following sense) but on his independent judgment and the ingredients that go into that judgment.[7]

In talking about a person, as we saw before, it is hard to separate action from character and in the last phrases quoted above "independent judgment" is what is being spoken of. Then, coupled with "the ingredients that go into that judgment," reference, I believe, is to what we have been calling "character" here. As a person Bill Jones' capacity to act, his own character and the character of the corporation combine to produce corporate action. We refer to this complex when we say "the corporation did so and so."

Now let us look at what is involved when "so and so" turns out to be wrong. Either an agent or a group of agents produced the action in question and, for simplicity, let us suppose a single agent. If the character of the agent's action in the main exhibits direct self-interest then he has neglected his duty as agent in favor of himself and is morally responsible for so doing. In reviewing the situation, the corporation may feel that it was partly responsible because, on the basis of past events, steps should have been taken to guard against such action. These steps may concern indications of this particular agent's character and potentially of all other agents or they may concern kinds of situations in which agents find themselves. In either case, corporate character needs modification as well as, of course, the possible removal of that agent. The point is that those modifications of character are the responsibility of those who occupy the relevant positions in the corporate hierarchy; it is, of course, this concern for the character of the corporation as well as its expression that is the primary function of management and the moral dimension is neither something extrinsic nor added to this management function but arises out of the full recognition of the conditions required for the shepherding of responsible practice. When a person accepts a corporate office he becomes morally responsible for the part of company character under its authority and influence and that includes not only policy by previous occupants but for what ought to be but has not yet been done.

In the light of the above considerations I cannot see attributing moral agency to what are, I believe, the conditions of moral agency as Professor French's paper seems to. Nor do I see the need for the projection of the moral onto the corporate as Professor Goodpaster's paper suggests. What is required is the recognition of the grounds for the application of an analogy between individual persons and corporations on the basis of the distinction between character and action and the moral significance of this distinction and its application.

From the perspective taken here, developing an institutional framework of ethical responsibility is directly possible in terms of the conditions of corporate character that shepherd responsible action by corporate agents. But it is only indirectly possible with regard to the actions taken by agents, themselves, for the corporation. Certainly, this is why what a corporation needs most is good management—and I am using 'good' in the moral sense developed here—a management that will shepherd corporate practice in the best possible ways.

In summary, I have wanted to mark-out corporate character as the legitimate ground for one very important kind of moral judgment and distinguish such moral judgments of character from moral judgments of activity. The development of corporate character is the primary moral responsibility of management because character shepherds the capacities for action of corporate agents. Even though management is a plurality, hierarchically ordered, at its best a corporation resembles the self-governing status of an individual person at its best, but of course, it is not an individual in the same sense. Rather, it is an organized and self-organizing collectivity, to use Professor French's term in a sense in which he may have meant it in his article. Viewed in this fashion, moral, responsible, self-governing action, both individual and corporate, will be consistent with its own possibility and does not need to be postulated or projected from the outside but arises within the corporate context through recognition of what is required in the interaction of corporate character with the capacities of its agents. Responsibility for action is always individual but the conditions enabling responsible action are a function of corporate character. Character is the responsibility of management.

Footnotes

1. Cf. Machiavelli's comments on the character of Soderini.

2. *Ethical Theory and Business*, Beauchamp, T. L. and Bowie, N. E., Eds., Englewood Cliffs, NJ: Prentice-Hall, Inc., 1979, pp. 175-86.

3. Ibid., p. 182.

4. Ibid., p. 178.

5. Ibid., p. 185.

6. Vol.2, No.1, 1983, pp.1-22.

7. Ibid., p.5.

Conclusion

CHAPTER 10

This work was begun to explore several questions: (1) What is the relation of traditional ethics and morality to the business activities of corporations? (2) Can corporations be held morally responsible for their practice? (3) What are the foundations of moral responsibility or Why should anyone be moral, let alone the corporation? It seemed to me that if moral considerations are basic for business then we should be able to be clear about why they are. It didn't appear satisfactory to impose "social responsibility" or "Judeo-Christian conscience" upon business activity from the outside, so to speak. If morality is important for business it should find its importance located in its own nature, within its own practice. Only then could the immoral be an instance of bad management where it belongs. Only then could the moral be seen to pervade all business studies and to be taken seriously by the schools of business. Oddly enough it isn't the business people out in the world who need to be convinced. They run into moral considerations in practice all the time. It is the people in the business schools teaching the next generation that pose the biggest problem. It is not merely because many faculty are set in their ways or because of the ways business has been traditionally thought about and taught. A good deal of that does exist. The real problem is that it amounts to a gigantic job of re-education in that field. This isn't easily done and above all it is not at all clear how to go about it without disturbing that "value-free" body of theory optimistically labelled "management science." There is no intent on my part to denigrate that body of theory in any way. It does what it does and stands on its own feet, but with regard to the overall context of business practice there are surrounding considerations that cannot be ignored any longer. Because of the increased importance of the economic dimension in our lives and because of the increased complexity of that dimension and the size of the corporations that are the chief actors in that dimension, a larger framework of concern and orientation is required. As has often been the case before, the point being made is exemplified in the development of theory in physics. The equations expressing Einstein's theory of relativity go beyond the equations for Newtonian mechanics. But the relation of the former to the latter is such that if you allow certain variables in Einstein's equations to equal zero then Newton's equations are derived. Before Einstein, certain aspects of physical reality weren't even recognized. Now we are aware of those aspects but under certain conditions can let them equal zero and apply the Newtonian framework usefully. I think there is an analogy here in what is happening in business. We may not have mathematical equations expressing the broader framework in which business is beginning to act. Perhaps we never will. But we are increasingly aware of these broader aspects and that means becoming increasingly aware, when we apply a cost-benefit analysis, for example, that certain of these broader aspects are being allowed to equal zero and to question whether in fact such allowance is appropriate. The canceling out or letting equal zero of such aspects has quite often been the cause of governmental attempts to regulate the practices of industry as well as of consumer distrust of business in the past hundred years. In the absence of a complete parallel in the disciplines of physics and business and such a condition, if possible, must await a theoretical rapprochement between biology and physics, business practice appears to be an art of judgment rather than a science in the strict sense.

In order to set forth the constraints present upon such an art, an analysis of the characteristics of activity or practice in general and business practice in particular was carried out because that is the context wherein responsibility is both desirable and problematic. That analysis brought to mind several characteristics of activity that are commonplace for reflection. The most significant of which are that activity is purposive, requires choice and has presuppositions. These presuppositions are the conditions without which activity could not come about. The setting forth of the enabling conditions of practice is significant for our search for the foundations of moral responsibility for a number of reasons all germane to the common and usual way business practice is thought about. In the first place the prominent saying that the bottom line in business is profit is just not true unless you include an "all things being equal" caveat and never inquire into what those "things equal" must be. Several authorities in business management, including Peter Drucker, have maintained that profits are not the goal of business but the instrument for measuring success or failure in your business. There is much truth in this way of looking at profits, but it does not bring out the two levels and dual focus of practice; one, the fulfilling of the goals of your practice, the other, the maintenance of the conditions which enable you to continue practicing with that goal or any other in mind. The real point, involved here, however, is that even the much heralded self-interest of the individual in business or any other practice requires these enabling conditions in order to operate. Because you have choice it is perfectly possible to destroy these conditions in your own choosing. Therefore no matter what goal you are pursuing not only must you do what is needful to attain it but, in the doing, you must not undercut those enabling conditions. To do your business calculations solely in terms of profit maximization is terribly short-sighted and inadequate.

In the second place is the fact that the conditions enabling you to practice are the same conditions that enable anyone else to practice. When you maintain them for yourself, you maintain them for everyone else as well. Practice that continues to accomplish this is responsible practice and is constitutive of a community of persons. That is the only way to acquire that "margin of excellence" aimed at in the Borg-Warner statement of beliefs quoted earlier (p. 63-4). I suspect that it is easy for people not far removed from frontier conditions to forget about enabling conditions. Toynbee somewhere points out that in the seventeenth and eighteenth centuries only two locations in the world enabled a family to support themselves on a limited amount of land, the east coast of America and the region just south of Moscow. That thought suggests the presence of enabling conditions in the ecological sense at least but also the personal qualities prized by Locke and our ancestors in the new world. You were free to operate within them and they became self-conscious in a degree in our New England town meeting tradition. Of course, it was wholly obvious that neighbors with the same sense of practice were of more help than anything else and could help maintain, and even reconstitute in barn raisings, ones enabling conditions. But as the frontier closed, land disappeared and the size of the population and interdependence of its people grew, the enabling conditions could no longer be taken for granted and ignored in our living as a people. The civil rights movement has been a partial recognition and bringing to consciousness of these conditions of free responsible practice but even there, they are not understood generally as the conditions of all our being as persons. We bemoan our loss of the sense of community and reach out for all manner of sources from which such community can be derived. My suggestion is that even though you may want to engage in commitment of some sort, as exemplified in the many examples in *Habits of the Heart*, a common foundation for concern for other-regarding motives conducive to community can be found in the conditions which enable our rightly prized individualism. In not taking account of these conditions in our practice our individualism has not been operating with a "full deck" to borrow a contemporary and telling phrase. But now the question of upon what authority do I make these pronouncements must be considered. Our forefathers would have said the "light of reason," but since then reason has come in for harsh treatment until it is almost coin of the realm that humans are not rational animals as Aristotle and the founding fathers supposed. And here I can only begin to tread on controversial ground but will try to consider the relevant aspects without overstating the case.

The traditional understanding of what is revealed by the light of reason is the truth, plain and unvarnished by human bias. I believe that understanding of the deliveries of reason has been dealt sufficient body blows to damage our faith in it. There is the general perception that all truth is relative or biased and, more technically, that all assertion involves interpretation, the denial of what was once known as the possibility of objectivity. All truth is within a system or ideology and there is no eluding this condition. This skepticism has to do with what is traditionally called the theoretical use of reason. That is why I have stressed the primacy of practice throughout because it seems to me that the practical employment of reason is prior and self-standing. In the absence of any self-evident truths that are not dependent for their certainty upon some systematic criteria, such as the numbers system for 2 + 2 = 4 or the system of meanings for logical truth, I have come to regard the deliverance of practical reason as the only certainty of which I am aware. It may be objected that I am only substituting a system of practice for the numbers system in mathematics, the logical system or some other ideology. If that is true, then my only justification for taking the certainty of the system of practice more seriously than any other system is because the system of practice seems to involve, at least to some degree, not only my thinking about practice but the world in which I practice. There is something more than ideology involved in practice. The conditions in the world participate directly, and not merely hypothetically as in theory, in my practice. I say "my practice" purposely, because what I have been putting forth is not just a theory of practice. That would be unsatisfactory simply because the ethics as a theory would have no "bite," no underpinning for the "ought," apart from the context of practice. I believe that in practice I am in direct touch and commerce with something other than myself. The subject-object split does not apply.

Practical reason is a reflective capacity, traditionally taken to be intrinsic to the philosophic point of view. Kant, who was the first modern to assert the primacy of the practical over the theoretical use of reason reserved knowledge for the theoretical in answer to Hume's skepticism and denied to the practical any acquisition of knowledge. Practical reason's concern was with the determination of the ends of practice. Not only am I not bound by the needs of a Newtonian nature as Kant took his phenomenal world to be, but I can't see any grounds for thinking about practice in a certain way unless some justification can be given for so thinking in practice itself. And this is what the reflective use of reason seems to afford. How is this accomplished?

In reflecting upon practice, we begin with the description of the elements characterizing practice (the fifteen elements in Ch. Two). That activity of description itself is an example of what is being described. One of the elements of that reflective description is that practice has presuppositions, conditions in the absence of which practice could not come about. That element along with the element of choice exercised in practice suggests the criterion that a practice should be consistent with its own possibility and that those enabling conditions function as norms in our practice to be ignored at our own peril as expressed in the pragmatic contradiction. From the time of Parmenides through Leibniz and down to our own, the convinced rationalist of the theoretical kind has held the law of non-contradiction to be of central consideration for philosophy, but if thinking or philosophizing is seen to be a species of practice then the pragmatic contradiction becomes central to the human enterprise of thinking, philosophizing, sciencing, business practice or whatever. The implications of this displacement can not be pursued in the present context. However, their importance in an ethic of practice and for our criterion of right and wrong or just and unjust practice should be clear. But just what is the status of these enabling conditions? Are they items of knowledge? Quite obviously they are not the kind of knowledge delivered by the several scientific disciplines. There is no hypothesis and verification procedure. Instead, for practice of the kind I am engaged in as I write this to be possible, I must possess in sufficient degree the capacities of choice, concern and consistency and be writing in a world possessing in sufficient degree multiplicity, continuity and structure. These conclusions come from reflection upon what must be the case for me to be doing as I am doing. You can say that they are the presuppositions of practice. But can it be said that we know we are free? Not in any ultimate sense. In so far as human beings are able to confirm these enabling conditions in their practice they bring about states or conditions of being such as freedom, responsibility and personhood that would otherwise not exist. Only then is individualism a reality. Unless the capacity to practice is actualized at least to some degree in human beings they are something less than fully human and more nearly just highly complex animals; expressed in Sartrean terms, less fully "pour soi" and more nearly "en soi." It would seem that the deliverances of practical reason do give us knowledge about the conditions of practice as we have described what we are doing. If this be knowledge only within the system of practice, as some might contend, then this is the practical system out of which all other theoretical systems take their bearings and genesis. But the point for us at present is that as a practicing human being these enabling conditions can be reflectively seen to be categorically imperative for my doing in the same way that the imperatives of thinking, the norms of identity, excluded middle and non-contradiction can be seen to be categorical and unconditioned for thinking. It is being in practice that occasions their normative character in both cases. Outside of the context of practice, there is nothing that I ought to do. But within the context of practice there are constraints operative upon my practice. Should some say they do not see the necessity of these norms, the reply is that like the skeptic they are caught in a pragmatic contradiction; the presuppositions of their assertion are inconsistent with the content of their assertion.

Of course, unless they perceive the necessity the reply will have no meaning for them. I can only refer back to the examples given in these pages.

Early in the introductory Chapter, three levels of practice were indicated beginning with the corporate level that includes the managerial level that, in turn, includes the individual level. In this work, the analysis and discussion has ranged indiscriminately over all three levels and what aspects of the ideas set out apply to which levels needs to be made clear.

The categorical, moral imperatives apply only to the individual person as individual. Only individuals can practice and come under the enabling conditions as necessary norms. The individual through choice can commit himself to the goal of managing and that goal places the individual under hypothetical imperatives pertinent to that goal. The individual may also choose to manage for a certain corporation and that institutes another set of hypothetical imperatives pertaining to the goals of the corporation for the individual. The latter two commitments are grounded in and rest upon the capacity of the individual to be responsible in his practice and that moral dimension has to permeate the other levels of commitment. As pointed out in Chapter Nine, an individual, as a top level manager for a corporation, must be concerned that the foundation of the moral level of individual practice is maintained throughout his organization. Only in this way can the agents who practice for the organization attain the margin of excellence as individuals necessary for successful corporate practice. The levels of managerial and corporate practice presuppose and build upon the level of individual practice. The categorical, moral concern for the enabling conditions of individual practice includes the three inner conditions of any practicing self as well as the external conditions affecting that practicing because the multiplicity, continuity and structure of the world have a direct relation to choice, concern and consistency. The concern in general may be categorical but, in any particular instance involving some goals, that concern will be in terms of consequences affirming the enabling conditions in appropriate ways. Thus, prudence takes its rightful place among moral concerns in an ethic of practice as does a justification for the moral concern for consequences. And where the demands of a given situation are at odds and do not allow a just practice, the categorical concern puts the individual on the spot, morally, when a judgment is required. Then the individual makes the best moral judgment he can and defends it as well as he is able.

There are to my mind two primary reasons recommending at least something like the orientation taken here.

The proposed criterion of just and unjust practice as being or not being consistent with its own possibility is not formally empty. It refers directly to a definite condition in practice and reflects as nearly as I can make it the conditions which arise for a creature who is aware of being aware in practice, and who is continually subjecting that practice to criteria to govern its conditions and outcomes. Any theory of human behavior which does not account for and contain as a possibility these reflective capacities of humans is inadequate on the face of it. No matter what contemporary science says, and its assumptions about its subject matter have more often than not taken no account of these reflective possibilities, it just doesn't have anything interesting to say about human behavior that is fully human. Most often it cannot even account for its own theory. This began with generalizations on Newtonian mechanics and persisted throughout the modern period in the name of science and under the name of naturalism. Herewith, as nearly as I can reflect it, is a "naturalistically" oriented description of human behavior that can account for itself. If it goes beyond what is allowed in the naturalism generated by the scientific concern for other aspects of our experience, then let us recognize this fact and realize that their descriptive theories presuppose something like the position taken here in order to account for their own possibility. This leads to the second reason.

At both its best and its worst we emphasize our individualism and yet our science and technology and our cost-benefit analyses in business and our utilitarianism in ethics take no account of and pay no mind to individuals except as aggregates. No wonder we can find no grounds for individual commitment or responsibility if we think about our practice in those ways. Even the traditional discipline of ethics seems to suffer in the same fashion; an adequate system of ethics, deontological or consequential, would yield rules sufficiently general to cover all practice. If that is what ethics aims at, then, the degree of success attained is the degree to which we no longer need the individual as anything other than a rule governed mechanism. The orientation of these essays keeps the individual in business as the only viable, creative as well as error prone, creature we have. Practice is hinged and requires moral judgment that may be wrong when all is said and done. The responsibility is individual and lies with individuals. But much can be done to aid individuals in this task, not the least of which is an idea of practice that takes account of that possibility.

In Chapter Two, the twelfth characteristic (p. 15) reads

> Business practice requires the distinction between the *ideal and the real*; errors occur and ideally they should not. Practice must recognize the difference between what is and what ought to be.

Should the question arise as to whether, in what has just been said, we were dealing in facts or in ideals, the only answer, for anyone immersed in practice, is both. This is so because in practice I am dealing with things other than myself and subjecting them to interpretation and judgment appropriated as my own for the occasion. I am, then, living in the gap between the ideal and the real. That is the only possible location for a free and responsible individual and the only possible context for a meaningful world.

Index